How to
Think
Like a Fish

Also by the author

Somewhere Down the Crazy River:
Journeys in Search of Giant Fish (with Paul Boote)

River Monsters:
True Stories of the Ones That Didn't Get Away

How to
Think
Like a Fish

JEREMY WADE

DA CAPO PRESS

Da Capo Press
Hachette Book Group
1290 Avenue of the Americas, New York, NY 10104
dacapopress.com
@DaCapoPress, @DaCapoPR

Printed in the United States of America

First published in Great Britain in 2019 by Weidenfeld & Nicolson,
an imprint of The Orion Publishing Group Ltd.

First Edition: May 2019

Published by Da Capo Press, an imprint of Perseus Books, LLC,
a subsidiary of Hachette Book Group, Inc. The Da Capo Press name
and logo is a trademark of the Hachette Book Group.

The Hachette Speakers Bureau provides a wide range of authors for
speaking events. To find out more, go to www.hachettespeakersbureau.com
or call (866) 376-6591.

The publisher is not responsible for websites (or their content)
that are not owned by the publisher.

Da Capo edition editorial production by Christine Marra,
Marrathon Production Services. www.marrathoneditorial.org

Library of Congress Control Number: 2019934696

ISBN 978-0-306-84531-4 (hardcover), ISBN 978-0-306-84530-7 (ebook)

LSC-C

10 9 8 7 6 5 4 3 2 1

To M, M and C

There are but
Five notes
And yet their permutations
Are more
Than can ever be heard.

Sun-tzu, *The Art of War*

'Will you walk into my parlour?' said the
Spider to the Fly.

Mary Howitt, 1828

Contents

Contents

RIVER

DELTA

SEA

SOURCE

Going Under

There's something reassuring about low light and weight of water, and this place is one of the safest, deepest holes in the river. Down here, my eyes register the difference between night and day, but not much more. I move by touch, plotting my path on the map of memory. Not just the feel of rocks and sand and mud and weed but also the slip and scrub of the water. Far from being a uniform flow, it moves in different directions and at different speeds. This gives the river a distinct pattern, a grain – complex but logical, invisible but perfectly readable – which subtly encodes the position of the obstacles that shape it. This is why, even when I'm not touching anything solid, I always know where I am.

I nose into the place I was looking for. Close to my left side is a vertical rock wall, rising almost to the surface. If I were to reach out sideways with the tentacle on my upper jaw, I could touch it. Ahead of me is more rock, rising in steep steps, down which the water tumbles. I'm in the angle formed by these two rocks, my belly lightly bumping on the riverbed. Behind me the water shallows somewhat and spreads out into a pool, before funneling into a rock-strewn run. Back there, marking time in the friction-slowed water near the riverbed, and lurking on the edges of the flow, are other hungry fish, which would rather be in the place where I am now, if it were not already occupied.

What's special about this spot is that anything carried by the current will settle directly in front of me, in the deep residual turbulence of the waterfall, where I can investigate it with minimal effort. And it appears that something is already here. The familiar smellscape is colored by tendrils of something else. I edge to my right and the scent gets stronger. My tentacle finds its source, and easing closer I confirm that it's a dead fish, its scales reflecting the almost non-existent light. It's fresh and succulent, but something about it troubles me.

Earlier today I saw one of the large shapes slide across the surface. I heard its high-pitched whine before I saw the silhouette. I've seen these before and I know they are dangerous. A couple of times, shortly after one passed, I've seen a red-tail fish twisting unnaturally and rising in the water, sending out its chemical alarm. So I back away and leave this meal, which looks too much like a gift. But I stay close enough to deter any competitor from darting in.

When I check on it later, the dead fish is still there. This is reassuring. I move up close and open my mouth, creating just enough suction to lightly pick it up. It moves freely, not appearing to be tethered. I back off a short distance and then drop it, and as I do so it appears to get caught in a tongue of current, fluttering up then obliquely down, before sliding to a rest right at the base of the rock face.

It doesn't move anymore, and I have the taste of it now, urging me to throw off any remaining caution. I wait and watch, inching closer, then open my mouth fully to suck it right in. As I do so, I double my body to the right, to turn my head downstream.

Sixty feet above, on a slanting rock beside the river, an electronic buzzer sounds and a dim green light shows thick nylon line rolling off an improbably large reel. Hands reach down and pick up the rod, then push the drag lever forward. With the spool now locked, the growing tension in the line starts to transmit in both directions. What happens now could determine how this ends. Not enough of a pause and the strike may not set the hook; too much and the bait may be ejected. So there's an instant of intense weighing and calculation, before the rod pulls up and back – and is wrenched down in response.

It's the moment this creature, which until then had existed only in my imagination, becomes real . . .

— 2 —

Fishing in Mind

One day in 1999 a man pulled a gun on me in Brazil,
but the only time I've been shot was in England. I was
sitting on the ground at the edge of a small pond, legs pulled
up in front of me, with my arms wrapped around my knees,
when something ripped through the foliage some yards to
my right. It took a few moments to work out what it was. The
farmer was on the far bank, and he'd taken a shot at a coot in
front of me. He couldn't see me because I was underneath a
willow tree, obscured by its trailing branches.

All this had barely registered when a second shot ric-
ocheted off the water, this time just a couple of feet away,
having narrowly missed the bird, which was now squawking
in alarm. The next shot hit me in the right armpit.

Recalling this now I have trouble believing the reaction of
my much younger self. As a teenager I was pretty useless in
a number of respects, but there was nothing wrong with my

reflexes and I had a well-developed sense of moral outrage. But I just continued to sit there. Having verified that there was no broken skin under my thick camo jacket, I concluded that it was probably just an air rifle – which he didn't fire again.

At this point everyone who has heard this story assumes I must have been 'guesting,' as the quaint euphemism goes. But no – I was there legally, as a paid-up club member. So what was it? Why didn't I dive for cover and/or start yelling at the farmer?

What I have to remember is how seriously I took my carp fishing. I was in stealth mode, fishing close in, and I didn't want to add to the disturbance. But, more importantly, I had recently invented 'twig-hung crust.' And although it was possible – as happened with the jet engine and nuclear magnetic resonance spectroscopy – that somebody, somewhere else had come up with the same idea, I didn't want to draw attention to my field tests.

The challenge with the carp in this pond, which sits on the edge of a Suffolk village, was that they were very wary of floating breadcrust, which back then was everybody's go-to surface bait. Normally the carp here would ignore it completely, but where the willow branches trailed in the water they would sometimes seem curious. The trouble with a freelined crust, though – a hook on the end of the line with no float, weights or anything else – was that it would always drift out of this zone, whereupon it would receive no more attention. Trying the obvious alternative, a crust anchored in position by a running lead on the bottom, would spook the carp when they bumped into the line.

My wheeze was to position myself to the side of the willow's trunk and swing an underhand cast straight out, towards a partial gap in the semicircular curtain of branches. In the middle of this gap was a single dangling branch that stopped two feet short of the water, with a horizontal twig projecting. My aim was to cast the bait over this twig, then tease it back into a position where there was no line on the surface to alarm the fish. A belly of slack line between rod tip and twig would allow the bait to move freely if taken.

Now the bait stayed in the zone long enough for any patrolling carp to investigate. My position under the tree also meant less chance of attracting the ducks, which were used to being fed by people and could read any human actions that were bread related. What I hadn't reckoned with was that some of them could also read the minds of fish. On two occasions a duck spotted my bait at the precise moment when a dark shape was tilting up towards it. After pausing for a couple of heart-pounding seconds, I had to lift the bait then flick it clear of a lunging beak.

But even when there was no competition from these feathered pests, the carp were super cautious. They would leave baits alone for a long time – over two hours sometimes without touching it, just looking occasionally – long enough for a normal crust to become semi-liquid and fall off the hook. Only a tough piece from the base of a carefully chosen loaf, cut not torn to shape, so as not to fissure the leathery skin, was going to stand a chance. Then, when a carp finally did take the bait . . . it didn't really take it. It would hold it gently in the extremity of its mouth and start to move off – and then let go. Striking before it let go, I discovered, connected with nothing. Far from bringing quick results, my new technique simply confirmed what everyone said and believed back then: that carp were supernaturally intelligent and mostly uncatchable.

Then one day, a quarter-hour after casting, a carp passed then circled back. In the next five minutes it gently mouthed the bait three times, each time moving it about eighteen inches before letting go. Then, finally, it didn't let go. I tightened up and was answered by a powerful plunge. After playing it first in the open water beyond the branches, then at close quarters under the umbrella of foliage in front of me, I slipped the net under a twelve-pound mirror carp.

A few days later I got one more, 13lb 10oz, and that was my lot for that water that summer. But back then in the early 1970s, double-figure carp were a big deal, and these fish helped to confirm my transition from carp angler to carp catcher.

Looking back now, I am struck by two things: how much my fishing has changed since then – and how much it is the same. Not the same in the way of the gear I use, or the fish I go after, or the waters I fish – these things could hardly be more different – but the same general approach at the heart of it all. In this story from the dusty recesses of memory, I see a way of fishing that is recognizably a precursor of the way I fish today.

The only thing that's fundamentally different – something my younger self never expected or dreamed of – is that when I go fishing now, I have an audience. Or, rather, I have two audiences.

One audience is the small group of people on the bank behind me, who will tell you, if you ask them, that fishing is absolutely the dullest spectator sport on the planet, if you have to watch it in unedited real time. They are there because it's their job. Somehow they've got to turn an activity that mostly happens inside the protagonist's head into compelling visual entertainment. So while I am in a timeless zone of cosmic oneness with nature, which looks identical to being half asleep, they are watching the seconds drag by.

Sometimes, to help pass the time, they engage in hushed conversation. Once, while watching the sun sink below the far bank of the Zambezi, in Mozambique, they spent an hour discussing the relative merits of different condiments in sandwiches. At other times, they ask me questions.

'Why do you always fish with your finger on the line?'

'What made you pick this spot?'

'Why don't you do what the local fisherman said, and put more baits out?'

'Are you really serious when you say we should pack everything up, and come back later?'

Sometimes they ask because I appear to be doing something illogical, or because it looks like I'm wasting time. Or it's just simple curiosity, a desire to understand the arcane process of trying to summon a fish. Once in a while there's even a question that I should have asked myself, but didn't. Whatever prompts them, these questions are always challenging. Usually I can give some kind of answer, but sometimes I can't. Or I start to answer, but the mental trail, after a few promising turns, enters the non-verbal right side of my brain, a place as mysterious as the water in front of me. And I find myself doing a different kind of fishing. I know there's something there – I can glimpse it – but I can't grasp it.

The other audience is with me in a strange, disembodied, but equally real way. These are the people who see me on a screen, catching a variety of rare, large, and sometimes very difficult fish, from all manner of ponds, creeks, lakes, rivers, estuaries and sometimes oceans around the world. Many of these people also have questions, but of a different type. They are asking for advice. Often the questions are quite detailed – this species, that location – but they boil down to the same thing:

'Why do I just get small fish all the time? How do I catch the big ones?'

'What's your secret?'

The questions used to arrive by email, and in the early days, before the sheer quantity of messages, of all kinds, forced me to go electronically ex-directory, I would reply to everyone who contacted me. But again I struggled to know what to say, only this time it wasn't because of the inherent non-verbal nature of what goes on in an angler's head. The questions made me feel fraudulent.

The truth is, the kind of angling I do is very far from typical. And my knowledge, and practice, of the types of angling that most people do, these days, is pretty sketchy. The last time I did any amount of general coarse angling was in my teens, nearly fifty years ago. I last fished regularly for carp (and English wels catfish) in my twenties. I find this hard to believe myself, but the fork in the road that I took, in March 1982, to travel to far-flung waters after more exotic fish, was an all-or-nothing step. It didn't leave any surplus time or resources for anything else. So for most kinds of fishing that you care to mention, there are many people out there who would leave me standing. I'm very far from being an all-around expert, and I'm most definitely not a walking encyclopedia. What I do is very niche.

Specifically, until the last decade or so, my thing was making long expeditions, on the cheap and mostly solo, to places where other anglers didn't go – to catch fish that most people, back then, had never heard of: mahseer in India, goliath tigerfish in the Congo, arapaima in the Amazon. For this kind of fishing, the main achievement was getting back in one piece. Catching fish was a bonus – dependent on avoiding injury, illness and arrest, then having some last dregs of energy left to get a line in the water. Traveling could be painfully slow – sometimes two or three weeks just to get to the water, and the same to get out – and my gear was limited to what I could carry onto a crowded bus, truck or passenger boat. It couldn't have been further from the roach, chub and pike that started me on this journey.

Then came my pact with the machine that now follows me around, transforming a weightless part of me into a homunculus of dancing pixels. Although my more recent travels are (mostly) less seat-of-the-pants, and shorter in duration – three weeks normally, instead of two to five months – they have continued in a similar vein, having little or no overlap with most people's experience. And what this seemed to underline, when I started to think about it, was that I was uniquely *un*qualified to give any kind of fishing advice to anyone.

But then (when answering those emails) I thought about it some more. And although I couldn't make any specific suggestions about tackle and methods, for fish and places I knew nothing about, I found that I did have some things to say about another level of method. Not details of technique but general principles, which I've found to apply to pretty much any fishing situation. But then, again, I ran into problems. For each thing I started to examine, it was like trying to take a lure out of an untidy lure box, where the lure I was holding was hooked onto another one, which was attached to multiple others, which in turn were entangled with everything else around them. Then, as I contemplated this chaotic, spiky mass, I had a flash of insight. It occurred to me that I was looking at some kind of checklist – a mental program that is constantly going on in the background while I fish. But it was going to take more than a hopeful shake to separate the components.

The immediate temptation was to put the lid back on the box, and to keep on doing what I do, without trying to analyze it too much. This can, after all, carry the risk of destroying what you examine. (If you're ever losing at tennis, compliment your opponent by asking them to explain how they hit their backhand, then watch their technique fall apart.) But part of me was intrigued. Disentangling the process – the essence of how I catch fish, which I instinctively knew was a thing of surprising simplicity – was a challenge on a par with catching any of those fish. And if I succeeded, it would be a belated but fitting response to my many questioners – the shot in the arm, perhaps, that many of them want. As such, it might even result, here and there, for novices and old hands alike, in helping to turn a monster of the imagination into reality.

This book is my attempt to display the contents of the box.

— 3 —

Art Meets Science

When I left school I was all set to go to art college, but it fell through at the last minute. That's why, a year later, I ended up studying for a zoology degree. This led to a brief career as a science teacher (I got out because my working day ended, on average, at 1.30 a.m.), but I have also, now and then, taught art classes. So I have my feet in what some people regard as two very different camps. But I don't see it that way at all. Science and art aren't mutually exclusive. The best science is creative, and great art has a deep logic, speaking a language that resonates with our innermost workings.

There's another common belief, sometimes manifesting as fear, which holds that analyzing something magical can only demystify it. But again, I don't agree. You can throw as much science as you like at the question of where we came from, but the mystery of the natural world and the wider universe is limitless.

And so it is with fishing. Fishing is defined by uncertainty. Even today it's little wonder if some people quietly believe that catching a big fish is a matter of waiting for the planets to come into special alignment. Or suspect, maybe, that the person who charms a monster must have made a pact with the devil. As with the wider universe, however, a scientific approach brings understanding. But we need have no fear that science will demystify it, and take away its soul, because no amount of analysis will ever get to the bottom of it. For this reason I have no worries about trying to get analytical about my fishing. Far from spoiling my time by the water, I believe this can only enrich it.

In fact, the kind of fishing I do has forced me to get analytical. This is because some of the places I go to have never been fished with a rod and line – there's no tried and trusted method to fall back on. I've had to go right back to first principles. To do that, I've had to think about what those principles are. And what I have come to understand is this:

Looked at in a certain way, catching a big fish is very simple. All you have to do is put the right bait in the right place at the right time. You could even express this as a formula: $B + P + T = F$. Of course there are many different possibilities for each of these three elements, and the number of ways you can put these multiple possibilities together is astronomical, but there is something about seeing the problem in these terms that makes it less daunting. When the big, overwhelming thing is broken into smaller elements, the mind can get to work.

But this is only the first part of the process: it only brings us to the moment when the fish takes the bait. The opportunity must now be converted into a result. Doing that successfully also depends on a number of things, which can again be listed. This time it's a longer list, much of it about the right gear, but each thing is more clear cut and more manageable. There's less excuse for getting it wrong. In fact I'd go further, and say there's no excuse for losing a fish at this point, if that is through human error. If an angler has really thought about this second part of the process in full, then the likelihood of getting the fish in, once it has taken the bait, should be very high. But if just one component of this second part has been neglected, then the far harder achievement of tempting the fish to the bait could all be for nothing.

So there's a hard part and an easy part – or a relatively easy part. Tempting and landing. To catch big fish intentionally, rather than by happy accident, every component of each part needs to be addressed. That still gives us a lot to think about, but the problem now starts to have a shape. It's something we can work on: a mental framework, or a checklist, or a formula, however you choose to visualize it. What was once a problem of such magnitude that it threatened to paralyze our thought processes can now be addressed with a clear head.

Recently I was locked in a small room with four other people and we had an hour to get out. This wasn't as traumatic as it at first sounds – it was one of those games for corporate team-building – but there's still something about being in a confined space with a clock ticking that concentrates the mind. Inside the room were a number of locked boxes, a locked cupboard, a selection of other objects and a second locked door, which we assumed was the way out. Most of the locks were combination padlocks, but there was also a dial lock, a keypad, and others that were more arcane. Clearly we needed to get opening those locks – but how? The simplest locks had three rotating barrels, so we were looking for one correct combination out of 1,000 possibilities

(000 to 999). I used to be able to open bike combination locks by feel, but modern locks are more robust, plus I'm out of practice since I left school. So forget that. Another possible strategy was to work through all the options for each lock (000, 001, 002 . . .) but even at the rattling rate of one combination per second that's potentially fifteen minutes for just the simplest lock. It was beyond obvious that this would never get us out in time. The other possible strategy was to investigate our environment for clues. Picking up a statue on a shelf, we found a key underneath it. This opened one of the boxes, which contained a document, on which were some numbers . . . After half an hour of shouting and sweating, we had several of the locks open and were well on our way to escaping. Then we discovered that the second door just led to another room, containing yet more locked boxes.

Did we get out in time? Not quite. We failed by eight seconds. But if we'd been working our way through random combinations for each lock, rather than looking around us and thinking things through, we'd still be there now. Yet this unthinking approach, of proceeding mechanically without looking for clues, as if there were all the time in the world, is common in fishing. And it can seem to make sense, because once in a while, as with playing the lottery, somebody some-where, out of all the countless participants, gets the result they hoped for. But for most that result never comes.

To do better than this, to fish with a realistic expectation of catching a big fish, it is necessary to gather information and feed this into the decision-making process. The more information, and the more intelligently this is handled, the greater the chance of success. Ideally every single aspect of how you fish should be considered: not just choice of tackle and method, choice of bait, and choice of where to present

17

the bait, but also a number of less obvious items that are not normally considered at all, and deeper layers of detail. Some of these other things can be crucial, the difference between success and failure. So nothing should be left at a default setting, unless there is good reason.

But all this takes energy. In practice it's much easier to fish with a large chunk of what we do on a lazy 'auto' setting. To do better, we first have to recognize that by following such an approach we're settling for less than optimum results. Then, to make the shift from there, to fishing in a way that is truly effective, we have to really want that big fish. But what does that even mean? How do we do that? Personally, I try to fish as if my life depended on it.

I know this sounds rather extreme, a bit airport-book-motivational, for a pastime that's supposed to be a rest from the hamster wheel, but bear with me. In the escape room there was a sense of urgency. Even though it wasn't a real life-or-death situation, the adrenaline was flowing almost as if it was. And the effect of adrenaline is to boost the supply of fuel, in the form of dissolved glucose, to the muscles and brain. It awakened memories of the kind of nerves I used to get in exams, bordering on panic. But panic is a sign of failure to deal with a crisis. It's precious energy being squandered on pointless activity. And if you don't channel some of that energy into mental processing of the situation, you're done for.

I once got lost in the Amazon jungle, with no compass, no GPS, no food and no water. At the time, I was based in an isolated hut a long way from the river, a simple raised platform with no walls and a palm-thatch roof, next to a hole in the ground that served as both bath and drinking water supply. Contrary to most jungle-explorer mythology, the people scattered along the riverbanks weren't all drug traffickers trying to kill me. I'd spent a lot of time learning some Portuguese before I came here, so I was able to decode their menacing-sounding mutterings, complete with waving machetes, as offers of freshly sliced watermelon. And, if I wanted it, a place to sling my hammock. José was introduced to me as a fisherman, but mostly he cultivated a clearing near his hut, on the edge of a hump of slightly raised ground. In the wet season this higher ground became an island and he could paddle all the way here, through the treetops, from the river. Now it was an hour-long assault course, balancing across log bridges, crossing a small lake by canoe, and wading through thigh-deep mud.

I paid rent in the form of occasional weeding and portering plus the odd fish or two from the small lake, to save José having to go there with his tattered gill nets. This gave him more opportunity to do what he enjoyed most, which was walking in the forest with his dogs and shotgun. Among the river folk, who mostly kept in sight of water, José was something of a legend. He would carry just three or four cartridges, and normally came back with the same number. But if there was a shot, he would be back with a paca, a curassow, or maybe a wild pig. Early in my stay, we dug out and killed an agouti from inside a hollow fallen tree. At the time this drawn-out and visible death made me sick to my stomach, but it was interesting, over the following weeks, how a monotonous and patchy diet dialed down my scruples.

On the day in question I was trying to get to a lake that I wanted to check out. José had given me directions, which at first made sense: follow the edge of the high ground, then just keep going. But very quickly the vegetation closed in and the way ahead became much more uncertain. The ground was now undulating in all directions and cleft by the beds of winding, dried-up creeks. I kept going for more than an hour as best I could, by which time I should have been at the lake. But I was not José, and by now I had no idea where I was. In role-reversal terms, it was like me telling him to borrow my car and drive up the motorway to London.

It was as I resolved to turn back that the full enormity of my situation sank in. My target now was not a lake a couple of miles long, but a single hut under the trees. Even if I'd known where I was and which way to go, just a degree or two out would have seen me missing my target and going past it – at which point there were a hundred miles of uninhabited forest before the Rio Madeira. It was even possible that I was on the wrong side of the hut right now. In fact, wherever I was, there was a whole 180-degree arc – basically any direction with an easterly component – that would take me into this zone. So I had a serious problem. Solving it was going to take some serious mental application, all the science and creativity I could muster.

The obvious answer was to head west, towards the river. Once there, I could look for José's moored boat, then pick up the path to the hut. If I didn't find it, I could follow the bank upstream, where there were some riverside huts that I might reach the next day. Downstream I had no idea how far it was to the nearest habitation. Or, if I was lucky, there might be a passing boat. But . . . I had no compass, and beneath the forest canopy I couldn't see the sun. How could I find out which way was west?

Often when things go wrong, my reaction is to swear a lot. Occasionally this has been filmed. Once the editor had to use the bleeping machine thirty-three times in the space of two minutes, but that was exceptional. On this occasion

I didn't swear. I seemed to know instinctively that I would be expending energy that I couldn't afford to waste. Instead I sucked some water from a muddy puddle, to replace the sweat that was soaking my shirt, and stuck my machete into an old, rotten tree trunk. Standing vertically, it cast multiple faint shadows, radiating like the spokes of a wheel, thanks to scattered small gaps in the canopy. But one shadow was marginally darker than the rest. This, I reasoned, must be pointing away from the sun – so either east or west, since I was pretty much on the equator. Which of the two it was depended on whether it was before or after midday. But I didn't have a watch . . .

I remembered sundials, and the fact that shadows are also clocks. So I marked the shadow's position and settled down to wait. Half an hour later the shadow had clearly lengthened, so it was after midday and the shadow was pointing east. As long as no clouds came over, I had a working compass.

I set off to the west, and little by little the trees became less dense and my horizons extended. After an hour the land started falling away to the north and I could somehow sense water. I decided to make a quick detour to investigate, and this brought me to a small lake. It was a worrying discovery, because I'd heard of no other lakes anywhere near where I was trying to go. Once there, however, I thought I saw more water in the distance, a certain brightness showing through the trees. Confident now of my navigation, but hearing distant thunder, I hurried in that direction. And as I reached the bank I saw the big island ahead of me; this was Lago Grande, the lake I'd been trying to find. I knew where I was.

Sighting on the furthest tree trunk I could see, I now set off quickly south, knowing that this course would bring me either to José's small lake or the path from the river. After

maybe an hour of navigating this way, taking repeated bear-
ings in brighter patches of forest, and always deviating to the
west if there was any difficult terrain, I came out smack in
the middle of the lake's northern shoreline. After traversing
the lake's boggy inlet, there was just enough light to follow
the path, which in that place is just a slight flattening of fallen
leaves. I arrived at the hut just before nightfall.

José laughed when I told him my story. 'If you hadn't come
back, I'd have gone out and found you,' he said.

Later, over boiled fish and gritty manioc, he told me about
two locals who had got lost in the same area the year before.
He mentioned, as if this was significant, that they'd had a
shotgun with them, along with two cartridges, some matches,
and the meat from a pig they had shot.

'How long did it take them to get out?' I asked.

Through a mouthful of fish bones he said, 'Twenty-two
days.'

The experience taught me two important lessons. Number
one: next time take a compass. Number two: adrenaline is a
powerful mind-expanding drug. Not only that, it's legal and
it's free. And while constant over-secretion is bad news for
your health if you're a harassed worker in a sedentary job,
injecting a little into our fishing could help to improve results. This won't be news to subsistence fishermen, for whom
the price of failure is going hungry. But an adrenaline-fueled
recreational fisherman sounds like a contradiction in terms
– until you think about it. That raised heartbeat, the feeling
of excitement at the waterside, is a sign that the adrenaline is
flowing. The thing now is to use it. Whenever I fish, I want to
apply that same degree of attention and thought that got me
out of the jungle.

And the magical thing about fishing is that we feel the

effects of adrenaline beside the humblest pond or stretch of canal. Even here we can learn to access those deeper layers of our potential, which we may never reach in other areas of our lives. It's heady stuff, and it's why we do it.

And when we turn our expanded attention to the challenge of catching a big fish, we can take heart from the knowledge that (as in the escape room and the Amazon forest) the hoped-for result *is* possible. If your target species is catchable on rod and line, then no individual specimen is uncatchable, given the right approach.

But I'm starting to get ahead of myself. When it comes to trying for a big fish, we should first make sure, as far as we can, that we are fishing in the right place.

— 4 —

The Importance of Being a Detective

When I first got into carp fishing, in my mid-teens, I
spent a lot of time not catching carp. Days and nights
with my eyes aching, staring at that piece of silver paper
hanging on the line above the reel, willing it to move. And it
scarcely ever did.

This was the 1970s, when carp in England were creatures
of mythology, only rarely materializing in the corporeal world.
People clocked up hundreds, even thousands, of hours by
the water without getting even a touch. Such spectacular
failure was almost something to be bragged about, a sign of
true devotion. It set us apart from those who fished for lesser
species, who didn't have the physical and mental stamina to
go after the near-uncatchable carp.

Later I discovered why I had such a slow start to my carp-
fishing career. Some of the waters I fished didn't have any
carp in them. I was fishing for rumors.

It was an early lesson in the importance of fishing the right place – as in the right water. And it's what happens, sometimes, when you fish where other anglers don't.

More recently, in 1993, I took myself to the Brazilian Amazon, on a mission to catch an arapaima (*Arapaima gigas*), which is often said to be the largest freshwater fish in the world. I'd done what research I could, but I had no clear destination. It hadn't been possible to narrow my search down to a specific place. In the end it wasn't quite sticking a pin in the map, but it wasn't far off. I settled on the Rio Purus, one of the Amazon's southern tributaries. The Purus is a 'whitewater' river, meaning it flows heavy with sediment from the Andes – which in fact gives it a milky-brown coloration. This is significant because, unlike the Amazon's clear-water and black-water tributaries, it is rich in the nutrients necessary for aquatic life. It promised an abundant ecosystem, all the way from swarms of biting insects right up to the fabled super-predator of the floodplain lakes.

My plan was to go as remote as possible, beyond the reach of the subsistence fishermen. To help me navigate the human environment, I had done three months of intensive language study – a solid three hours every day. And I was well prepared for the rigors and uncertainties of traveling that lay in wait, having made three expeditions to the much tougher Congo rainforest in equatorial Africa. So I was confident of success.

My three months in Brazil brought me a grand total of zero arapaima. I finally got a small one, four feet long and weighing maybe forty-five pounds, six years later, after going back every year in between.

In my defense, I caught lots of other fish, and I got sidetracked for far too long looking for freshwater dolphins and anacondas. But it's still failure on an epic scale. Based on this

I'm the last person who should be giving anyone any advice on how to fish – at least on where to fish. Or perhaps not, because there is an important point to this story.

Most of the Amazon, it turns out, is nothing like what we see on nature documentaries, where it seems you can hardly move without tripping over boa constrictors and jaguars. Unlikely as it sounds, there is a huge commercial fishing industry, much of it to feed the two million inhabitants of Manaus, the improbable city at the heart of the region. Countless boats, carrying tons of ice, make voyages of hundreds of miles up the winding tributaries – especially the Purus – catching fish and buying fish from locals. Back then, lack of ice and refrigeration in the remoter parts was no help to the arapaima, thanks to the market for their dried, salted flesh and the general lack of other ways for people to get cash. I remember asking José where I could find a lake where the arapaima fishermen didn't go. He snorted at my naivety and said, 'They get everywhere.'

I later saw just how true that was, when I made some sorties with a team of arapaima hunters. They were like guerrilla missions behind enemy lines, days on end going deep into uninhabited jungle, living off the river and a small supply of coffee, sugar and manioc flour. To reach lakes that had no access by water, we dragged the heavy wooden canoes through swamps and forest.

When they arrived at a lake, the fishermen would quietly watch to locate the arapaima, which surface at intervals of up to half an hour to gulp air. This behavior enables arapaima to keep hunting as water and oxygen levels fall – but it has become their Achilles heel. Then the nets were deployed, hanging like curtains from surface to bottom. If necessary the fishermen would dive down to clear and even saw through snags that might hold the nets off the bottom. Then they beat the water with sticks to drive the fish into the meshes. They also used harpoons to probe for fish that had learned to lie low and stay quiet. Fishing this way, if a lake is small and not too deep and snaggy, a team of netsmen can completely empty it of arapaima, everything apart from the baby two- and maybe three-footers, which slip through the mesh. It is tactical and ruthless, and it has to be seen to understand why a lone angler with a rod just can't compete, and why any rare escapees can be almost supernaturally wary.

So those faded photographs I'd seen, of barrel-wide arapaima harpooned from the Rio Purus, alongside beached manatees with their nostrils plugged to suffocate them, were only part of the story. Unlike non-existent carp, there was hard evidence for their existence in the past. But arapaima hunters don't catch and release. The fact that a lake, or a region, held arapaima in 1910, or even 1970, means nothing today.

These two experiences, with carp and arapaima, taught me a lot about the importance of research. I could have saved myself a lot of time, trouble and disappointment by only fishing waters where there had been documented carp captures. But on my arapaima hunt, there were no documented rod- and-line captures to go on – that was my whole reason for wanting to catch one. Looking back, conventional wisdom says I should have bailed out of the Purus sooner than I did, and tried elsewhere. Certainly when I did so, I found that arapaima in less pressured waters are normally much easier to tempt. But I find I have (almost) no regrets, because in this case my inefficient angling brought a level of understanding – of this emblematic fish and the state of its Amazon home – that I wouldn't have come to otherwise. There are times, it turns out, when angling is not the be-all and end-all, but a door to something else.

It's also true, of course, that it's necessary to experience some failure to calibrate our appreciation of success. Not enough failure should prompt as many questions as not enough success.

Nowadays, though, I don't have the luxury of time. If I don't get a fish I risk being out of a job. No fin no fee, as somebody, maybe me, once quipped. And that really concentrates the mind: I can't afford to go to the wrong place.

Of all the things I have to consider for the kind of fishing that I do, to bring about the magical convergence of right bait, right place and right time, place is the component with the widest range of possibilities. There's a lot of water out there, way too much to explore in a single lifetime, so it's a process of narrowing down. I start by researching the geographical range of my target species, as far as this is possible, in books and online, long before I go anywhere near the water. But this is only the start. Most big freshwater fish, in most parts of the world, have all but disappeared from most places where they used to live. As with arapaima, the main reason is over-harvesting, but there are other factors too. Dams block the migration routes of many fish, so they disappear from the water above the dam – or even altogether, if breeding grounds are cut off. Draining of floodplains, cutting off backwaters, competition from invasive species and pollution also play a part. And sometimes it's just willful slaughter, as was the case with North American alligator gar in the early 1900s, thanks to the incorrect assumption that killing these predators would boost populations of 'game' fish. Consequently it's a sad fact of life that most big fish now tend to be restricted to isolated pockets here and there, which can be hard to find.

To locate these special places, it's a matter of keeping one's antennas active, of tuning in to the buzz and whisper of the water people. It's a world of tip-offs and informants, of reading between the lines, of triangulating one source with another, to weed out the wishful thinking, the exaggerations and misinformation. It's about correlation and extrapolation, about building a meaningful picture from mere scraps and fragments. In other words, it's an extension of what I used to do when I was fishing in England: the same principles but with less information. Except sometimes there's so little information that it seems to shift into something else, more like astronomy. When I first considered going to Zaire, now Democratic Republic of Congo, in search of goliath tigerfish, the place was an information black hole. In the end there was no alternative to going in blind. It was a miserable two-month blank trip, but an invaluable recon. (I ended up in an area where it can be both dry season and flood season at the same time – work that one out! – with the fish dispersed throughout the forest and even netsmen going hungry. In other words: right place, wrong time.) Now though, after more than three decades of doing this kind of thing, in various far-flung corners, I'm in the happy position of having done the leg work, and the paddle work, and knowing the basic lie of the water. With this mental framework in place it's easier to extract meaning from new wisps of intel, and to set off with some degree of confidence.

Once on location, the narrowing down continues. I talk to people, and try to find reliable sources, to take me to a deeper layer of detail. So important is this that, even if I have a translator, I try to learn some basics of the language in advance, at least some greetings and key fish-related vocabulary. A little of this can go a very long way, thanks to the fact that fishing itself is a universal language. Wherever I go, the curiosity is mutual, and I invariably find a first-rate accomplice. Gaining trust, though, is a circuitous process and takes time. In places where they haven't seen rod-and-line fishing before, there's usually disbelief at first that my thin line is capable of catching the big fish I'm after. Then they see how my super-light gear works – how near-invisible line, rigged on a reel that yields and a flexible rod, can bring in an arm-sized catfish – and how my fine 150lb braid can present a bait in places and ways that aren't possible with a thick 300lb handline or a length of rope, and there's a eureka moment. Where this then leads, if I'm lucky, is to a collaborative process whereby we catch a fish that neither of us, working alone, would ever have seen.

In short, then, finding the right place is all about good information, about tapping in to local intelligence – particularly if time is limited. Only right at the end – the final zeroing-in of the cross-hairs and divining the coordinates in three dimensions – does it change, sometimes, into something else. But up until that point it's information, information, information, whatever kind of fishing you are doing.

Or you can ignore everything I've said and fish for rumors. A good angler studies the rules for the very purpose, sometimes, of breaking them. In fact there can be special delight in tearing up the rules and scattering them to the wind, because fishing is also about the power of hope, sometimes against all odds. And sometimes it is about the miraculous.

STREAM

— 5 —

Think Like a Fish

On a slanting rock beside the river, an electronic buzzer sounds and a dim green light shows thick nylon line rolling off an improbably large reel. Hands reach down and pick up the rod, then push the drag lever forward. With the spool now locked, the growing tension in the line starts to transmit in both directions. What happens now could determine how this ends. Not enough of a pause and the strike may not set the hook; too much and the bait may be ejected. So there's an instant of intense weighing and calculation, before the rod pulls up and back – and is wrenched down in response.

It's the moment this creature, which until then had existed only in my imagination, becomes real . . .

I was in Guyana, on the northern fringe of South America, fishing the Essequibo River. Although the rainforest here merges with that of the Amazon, the Essequibo is not part of the Amazon River system – but over geological time there have been connections, so it's home to many Amazonian fish species. I was here because, unlike most of the Amazon, the interior of Guyana hasn't suffered too much from commercial fishing. As a result this sparsely populated region is something of a wildlife refuge, and a highly promising location for hunting big Amazonian fish. Or at least that used to be the case. In the two years since I had last been here, things seemed to have changed.

The fish I was after is a solid, streamlined, shark-colored catfish that's capable of reaching astounding sizes. Ten feet long and 400 pounds is a realistic estimate of what might have lurked here and there in South America a century ago. But nowadays, thanks to decades of long lines and jug lines (baits fished under free-floating buoys), their numbers have crashed. The chances of encountering an outsize specimen are now vanishingly small.

In English this fish is known as the goliath catfish (*Brachyplatystoma filamentosum*), but it's known here as the *lau-lau*, and over the border in Brazil as the *piraiba* or *filhote*. The latter roughly translates as 'little one,' a back-handed nod to its potential size. (A decapitated five-foot slab in a fish market might be described to you as 'a nice little one.') On previous attempts on a couple of rivers I'd actually done quite well with this present-day rarity: I'd managed to catch a dozen or so. But they'd all been small, nothing much over a hundred pounds. On the Rio Araguaia in Brazil I'd once hooked something much bigger. But after towing the boat for several minutes, it set off on an eighty-yard run straight down – in water just thirty feet deep. As I struggled to process this, my boatman told me it must have gone under an illegal long line – a rope set across the riverbed, with shorter lengths at intervals bearing hooks. Eventually I got most of the line back in, but it then became clear I was never going to get fish plus rope to the surface, or to the bank. Since that day I'd been after a rematch with a big one.

But this time in Guyana the signs weren't good. Normally for an hour-long episode we like to get another fish species or two, besides our main target, as an appetizer for the main course, and in the past the Essequibo had been very obliging. A lure cast to the eddies below rocks would bring hits from peacock bass (actually not bass but large predatory cichlids) – but not this time. Locals told us that people had been arriving from way downstream, their boats full of ice-boxes, and heading back with fish to sell in the gold-mining areas. Not only that, the red-tailed catfish (*Phractocephalus hemioliopterus*) were strangely absent. Normally a dead fish put out for lau-lau would sooner or later get the attention of these plump, big-headed beasts – but not now. This was more mysterious. It seemed to be linked with the increasingly unpredictable ups and downs of the river level.

Some fish, like salmon, freshwater eels and most sturgeon species, are well known to make long migrations between fresh and salt water. What's less well known is that many other fish travel long distances entirely within fresh water. The record-holder, so far as anyone knows at the moment, is another Amazon catfish, the *dourada* (*Brachyplatystoma rousseauxii*). This looks just like a small piraiba (it only rarely exceeds a hundred pounds) but with a lighter, pale yellow coloration (hence the name, which means golden). Dourada spawn in the Andes, in the headwaters of the Amazon tributaries, and their larvae drift down to the Amazon delta, on Brazil's Atlantic coast, where the juveniles feed and put on weight for a couple of years before starting their journey back upstream. All the way up, they run the gauntlet of nets and lines. But of the fish that escape, those that make it to the furthest headwaters will have completed an underwater round-trip of 7,000 miles.

In contrast to this one-time, down-then-up migration, other species swim upstream to breed every year. In the absence of a calendar, they take their cue from the state of the river. But over the last couple of decades, fishermen in many parts of the world have told me that the seasonal ups and downs of river levels have become much more unpredictable than they used to be. It's certainly happening on the Essequibo, and some of the effects of this are visible. I've seen river turtle eggs, which had been buried in emerging sand beaches, washed away when the water unexpectedly rose again after a false start to the dry season. And if the turtles are confused, laying nests full of eggs that will never hatch, then who knows how this is affecting the fish? For whatever reason, it seemed that the red-tails just weren't there. And this stoked my fear that the lau-lau, which are known to make spawning runs far upstream, had vacated this stretch of river.

I thought back to when I'd arrived, and I'd seen the river five or six feet up on what it should have been. Even so, I'd been optimistic, buoyed by memories of the Essequibo's productivity, even when conditions weren't quite right. Methodically I'd set about fishing the deep holes and pools where lau-lau had been encountered in the past. Nothing. More time passed, with the same lack of result. Normally on a three-week trip I have three to five days allocated to catching the fish, but for this fish I'd always known it was going to be difficult, so I had pushed for eleven days. Even so, it was starting to look like I would run out of time.

A familiar question surfaced: stick or twist? Keep trying the spots the local fishermen recommended or try something new? I'd seen a place I liked the look of, but the locals were dismissive. It was a pool downstream of some rocks, but on a smaller scale than the more favored places, and I was told it wasn't very deep. I decided to check it out anyway, with the sonar I'd brought along. This is something I often travel with now: it gives me a basic depth map in my notebook much more quickly than a lead weight on a line. Working systematically I found a small area that was sixty feet deep, as deep as anywhere I'd found elsewhere – not in the middle of the pool but tight in one corner. I decided to fish here for the last couple of hours before dark, and by casting to a few different spots I got a feel of what the current did beneath the surface. One cast also produced a four-pound red-tailed catfish, which seemed like a good sign. I suggested that we come back again, and fish through the night.

My feeling was based on something that I do quite often. I try to imagine that I am a fish. And the first thing to understand about fish is that they are underwater accountants, instinctive experts in the management of the most elemental currency: energy. Their governing principle is very simple: overall income has to exceed expenditure. If it doesn't, they're struck from the book of life, simple as that. So they don't waste energy battling current unless there's a very good reason. That keeps energy consumption down, but they still have to find food. The smart way to do that, in a river, is to find a place where food is delivered to them. Normally that means some kind of slack or eddy. The other big consideration is safety. Such a place is no good if it exposes the fish to potential danger. So the ideal lie provides three things: comfort, food and safety. But such special places are valuable real estate; there's going to be competition to occupy them. And what tends to determine who wins and who loses out is that all-pervading natural law: might is right.

So if I were a fish, big enough to have my pick of all the places in that pool, where would I be? It seemed pretty clear cut: where the water tumbled into the deep hole. My place was sorted. As for bait, this would be the most succulent dead fish we could get hold of, ideally about two pounds in weight, with cuts to let the scent slowly dissipate. Time was the thing we had little choice over. It had almost run out. But I didn't want to fish the remaining 24 hours around the clock: I wanted to fish with full focus and alertness. I decided on night-time because if I were a fish, that's when I would feel safer.

Late next afternoon we were back. The rocks in the river, I noticed, now showed a distinct high-water mark well above the surface. The water was falling, which I took as a good sign. Any fish that might have moved upstream might have dropped back. Moving slowly and quietly, the crew disembarked onto a sloping slab of rock and took all their kit well back from the water. They'd heard it all before, but I made a special point of emphasizing stealth. I'd be fishing close in, and despite the noise of water pouring into the pool, even a single careless thud could transmit to a fish and ruin our chances.

Because of all the rocks in the water, I had geared up with 100lb monofilament line right through, with a short leader of 300lb braided Kevlar for the necessary combination of strength and suppleness at the business end. To hold enough line to cope with a big fish charging down the pool, I was using a massive saltwater multiplier (50lb-class, wide spool, long range), and to match this I was using a super-stout 6ft rod that a gentleman from Long Island, New York, had built for me for shore-based shark fishing.

By any normal freshwater standards (and most saltwater standards, for that matter) such gear is complete overkill. But I wasn't after a normal-sized fish, and this wasn't a normal fishing situation. The main thing here, because of the sharp rocks close in, was that nice, user-friendly braided line would have been nonsensical. Everything else followed on from that.

I ensured accurate bait placement by doing this from the boat – quite apart from the fact that casting with this gear would have been impossible. The bait was held in place by a 7oz weight attached to a sliding swivel by a short length of 18lb line tied with bad knots – so if the weight became snagged it would easily break free. Then I put out a second line, heavy braid this time, way down to the middle of the pool, 150 yards away. This was an insurance policy, or a gamble, depending on your point of view. I'm not normally a fan of extra lines, but in this case I reckoned that the pros of this outweighed the cons. With the baits out, we then moored the boat in position for an emergency boarding if necessary. If a fish didn't look like stopping, or became snagged, my boatman Neville would take me onto the water. Finally I set and tested my bite alarms, which transmitted to a receiver next to my ear. I told the crew to get some rest. They'd know soon enough if anything happened.

Night fell and the world quietened. I had a good feeling: not the certainty that I would catch a fish (which some anglers have a habit of remembering after the event) but certainty that I was doing everything right, or as right as I possibly could. I'd been through the mental drill, with each rod, of working out which hand would go where and in what order, should I need to pick it up and strike, and I'd repeated this in my head so I wouldn't have to think about it at the time. Imperceptibly I entered that special zone. I was simultaneously relaxed, wakeful and alert – a state of mind that is a tonic in itself, which we would all do well to enter more in everyday life, but which we rarely achieve. It's a variant of what's known in some martial arts as *zanshin*, a state of awareness and readiness, which isn't a normal default but something that needs to be cultivated. I knew that something could happen at any moment, which might be ten hours away or one breath away. But whenever it happened, it would almost certainly be my only opportunity.

At an unknown hour the buzzer stuttered into life and I was on my feet. It was the other rod going, the right-hand rod. Something had taken the bait in the middle of the pool. I picked up, engaged the drag to its pre-set strike setting, let the line tighten, pulled back – and felt the weight of a fish. But I could tell straight away it wasn't a big one. On the heavy gear I brought it in quickly and swung it ashore. It was a dark-colored catfish just a few pounds in weight, with its eyes near the angle of a deep-cleft mouth and a pair of half-inch tentacles recessed into the upper jaw. The disturbance caused by catching such a small fish was unwelcome, but with our low fish count to date it was worth getting a few quick shots before it went back.

It was while I was showing this fish to the camera that the other alarm sounded. I dropped the small catfish in the water and went to the big rod, but the run had stopped. Maybe it had spooked because of the movement on the bank. After a little while I pulled the line gently to see if I could feel the bait, and there it was. Or was it? I pulled some more and thought I could feel the weight moving, bumping along rock. I considered pulling the bait out to check it but decided to leave it, in a position that was now very close to the base of the drop-off.

Scarcely had I done this when the line started moving out again. This time it kept going, so I engaged the reel . . . then struck. The answering pull had me yelling for the harness and for getting the camera light out of my face – and on the verge of jumping in the boat. But the heavy gear did its job and stopped the fish building up momentum, and brought it, eventually, to a sulking halt. Then suddenly something wasn't right. It felt as if the line was grating on something, and the contact was no longer direct. But at least I could still feel, just, a force that was alive. I tried to process this information – line trapped in a cleft in a rock? – and think what to do. But then everything was viscerally direct once more, my body doubling in response to the lunges on the line. The pressure, however, was having its effect: the fish was grudgingly coming closer, and up through the water column. Then – maybe it touched the sunken lip of our ledge or it was the sight of our lights – there was a huge explosion on the surface that showered us all with water. My uncertainty now focused on the hook hold; almost everything depended on that. A couple more huge swirls had us straining to see it, while Neville stood ready with a rope to put around its tail, because our sloping platform would not be a secure place to hold a big fish.

When the moment came, Neville made no mistake. Immediately I put the rod down and grabbed the lower jaw. As the dark-grey body emerged from the water, a hushed voice from behind was heard to say, 'Oh . . . my . . . God!' A minute later we hoisted it in a heavy-duty sling and for the few seconds that it was clear of the ground a set of industrial scales recorded a weight, minus the sling, of 251 pounds.

Only after the fish was back in the water did we notice the blood. While holding up an LED light-panel to illuminate the action, our assistant producer had been attacked by night-flying wasps. The noises she'd been making while the rest of us had been impatiently shushing her had been her one-handed attempts to fend them off, and the sounds of suppressed screams as they stung her. The bleeding nose was from a self-inflicted punch, while the light continued to shine steadily on the other battle until its end.

It's a footnote that says something about dedication, the strong desire for a successful result, which is part of most fishing stories and part of what makes us fully human. But the defining part of this story, I think – the part that made the real difference – is the time I spent looking into the water, letting my mind drift, as I tried to think like a fish.

— 6 —

In Search of the Secret Ingredient

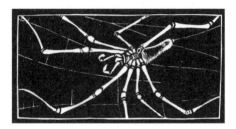

In the dry season the Luangwa River shrinks to a narrow ribbon in the middle of a wide, flat, sandy floodplain. Where the water deepens into pools, there are dense grey-and-pink archipelagos of sunburnt hippopotamuses, flicking their ears and laughing menacingly if you start to come too close. But this morning things are different. It rained during the night, and the river now has branches: small streams just a few feet wide, reaching through the gaps in the edge of the plain into the beds of ghost side-rivers.

I am walking along the sand when I see movement up ahead. Where one of these new streams bends and widens there is a ripple, which becomes a hump of water pushing upstream. It is a sizeable fish, long and sinuous, which barely has enough depth to swim. With stealth unnecessary, I run up to it, and see that it is some kind of catfish. As it continues to wriggle against the flow, I sweep a hand underneath its

43

middle (being careful to avoid its pectoral fins, in case it has sharp spines) and flick it onto the sand. It's the size of my forearm, maybe four pounds, and in the next half-hour I get two more.

As my head buzzes under the equatorial sun, I have a sudden realization. This is almost certainly how fishing started. Not only that, it's also *where* it started. I'm in eastern Zambia, in Africa, the continent where our two-legged ancestors split off from the four-legged great apes around six million years ago, and where modern *Homo sapiens* first arose, around 200,000 years ago, with their large brains and clever hands, before they spread around the rest of the world. The knowledge makes this catch momentous. And it makes me wonder. Was my predatory reaction to the sight of those fish because I am an angler, or because I am human? What's certain is that my African ancestor would not have put those fish back in the water, as I did. For somebody living hand to mouth, a fish in the hand, after weeks of drought, might be a lifesaver.

But the chance grabbing of a stranded fish, on its hopeful way to its once-a-year spawning, isn't going to come along very often. Early humans would have known that there were plenty of other fish in the water, but how to get them? This wouldn't have been just a matter of idle curiosity: there was a powerful incentive to be inventive, and to use their inventions effectively. And the measure of success was brutal. If the energy value of what they extracted from the environment was less than the energy expended in the process of extracting it, they would waste away and die. It's the same principle that Mr. Micawber famously summarizes in *David Copperfield*: if income exceeds expenditure the result is happiness, but if expenditure exceeds income, even by the tiniest amount, the result is misery. In the case of prehistoric hunter-gatherers, however, it was more than happiness versus misery: it was survival or starvation, literally life or death.

So necessity drove invention. It's easy to imagine how, at first, fishermen started using clubs and spears for fish that couldn't simply be grabbed. Then came harpoons for bigger fish, where a harpoon head made from bone or horn, complete with barbs and attached to a length of cord made from twisted vegetable fibers, broke away from the wooden shaft after impaling. The earliest known harpoon heads, carved from bone and most probably used for catfish, date from about 90,000 years ago, and were found in the southern Congo basin.

Then came an invention to target fish with better accuracy. Some years after my visit to the Luangwa River I was in the Solomon Islands, in the South Pacific. One of my tasks here was to shoot a mullet with a bow and arrow, up one of the mangrove-fringed creeks. I already had some experience with a bow, having shot a couple of peacock bass in the Amazon. The technique for this was to paddle a canoe through flooded undergrowth at first light and find the fish resting motionless at the surface. For somebody who can shoot accurately and get through the tangles quietly, they can be sitting ducks. The mullet were a different proposition entirely. This was because we hardly saw any. Standing in the bow of the wobbly canoe I let fly a few arrows at distant shadows but it looked like I was going to finish up empty-handed. Then I saw three fish arrowing out of the mangroves – four feet down, one behind another, blurring towards me diagonally right to left. I tracked ahead of the middle one, then slightly down to correct for refraction, and released. From the behavior of the buoyant arrow-shaft I instantly knew that I'd scored a hit. I could hardly believe it: one of my flukiest catches ever. And it brought a strange mixture of emotions: a dying fish in my hands but a feeling of accomplishment, and another frisson of connection across the millennia.

As fish-hunting inventions go, a sharp projectile fired with force has a certain predictability about it. But some techniques used by the islanders take some believing. Consider the *kuarao*. One morning I joined the men as they set off into a patch of forest, armed with machetes. For two hours they hunted and cut lengths of vine – a thumb-wide stem with long, narrow leaves every few inches – and joined them into a single super-vine a few hundred feet long. They then took one end and walked it into the waist-deep water of the reef, where it formed a green line on the surface, which extended and curved and eventually formed a circle more than a hundred yards across. At this point the women and children joined in, spacing themselves around the perimeter, as the two ends started to overlap, closing the circle down. As the process continued, the circle became smaller still, as the curtain of leaves became more and more dense and the people shuffled closer together. Then we could see them: a shoal of panicked fish, darting here and there around a small circular enclosure made from lumps of dead coral, with one gap in its wall.

The endgame was the final drawing-tight. Instead of swimming between the feet of the laughing, curly-haired children, the fish chose the perceived safety of the corral, whose door closed behind them. Then the spears rained down, and a canoe started to fill with the exotic colors of dead and still-flapping aquarium fish. When there were enough for the planned village feast, the rest of the fish were released.

The method works thanks to a profound insight into fish

psychology. If the vine were a net, it would immediately make sense, but there is no physical barrier to stop the fish getting out. Maybe the vine's shadow makes it seem more substantial than it is. Another theory is that the thin, flexible leaves make a rattling sound in the water as they move. Whatever the explanation, the other big question is: how did the islanders invent it? The answer must lie in the nature of the Solomon Islands. They are tiny scraps of unproductive land, which would have forced the inhabitants to extract food from the surrounding water, in whatever way they could. It's environment driving evolution, in this case not of species, but of fishing techniques.

It was also in the Solomons where I learned spider-web fishing. My tutor was James, a village elder with a gravelly voice, a permanent semi-smile and a faded blue baseball cap, who first of all gave me a small Y-shaped stick, like a catapult without the elastic. Having found the spider we were looking for, a mean-looking thing whose long black legs sported bulbous yellow joints, I carefully set about winding its tough silk across the arms of the stick. Then I held this in the heat of a fire and attached it to the end of a cord. Meanwhile James stitched together dried leaves into a dart-shaped kite, and we were ready to go. Out on the water we were greeted by a flat calm, but after a long paddle to the mouth of the lagoon we found a gentle breeze and a slight ripple. James launched the kite, and we angled our course so that the spider-web lure, dangling on its cord beneath the kite, tripped across the surface on a parallel track to the canoe. Suspended from the air, it was seemingly connected to nothing, and as we guided it out of the blue water into the turquoise shallows above the reef, the kite dipped, and James started slowly retrieving, hand over hand. All the while, now, he quietly whistled, clucked and talked to the fish that was flexing and splashing on the line. Then he reached into the water and grabbed the narrow snout of a two-foot needlefish. Its teeth were hooked and tangled into the web – the unlikeliest catch of any spider.

But the pressure to innovate was also strong elsewhere. Somewhere along the way early humans learned to make baskets, like the open-topped cones they still use in the Congo. You thrust this all the way down to the weeds on the bottom, then reach inside to see what you've got – and hope it's not an electric catfish. More sophisticated are basket traps, usually a large container with an entrance in the form of a funnel. The advantage of these is that you can set a number of them in the evening, along the edge of a river, with the opening facing downstream, and come back for your catch in the morning. They also found out about poison: dig up a root, such as the Amazonian *timbó*, beat it on a rock to release the milky sap, then jump in the water and collect the stricken fish at your leisure. And of course there are nets, originally made from woven vegetable fibers, knotted together. Seine nets hang from the surface to the bottom and are dragged by a team of fishermen to encircle the fish. Gill nets can be left to fish passively, catching fish whose size is determined by the size of the mesh. The earliest known net, found near present-day St. Petersburg, dates from around 10,300 years ago, but there must have been earlier nets that didn't get preserved.

And at some unknown point or points, fishing technology took a new direction. The first step in this direction was a device known as a gorge. This is a double-ended spike made of wood or bone, normally about three inches long, with a notch in the middle, around which a line is tied. This spike is threaded under the skin of a small fish, which is then thrown in the water, and if a bigger fish swallows this bait, a pull on the line frees the gorge, which gets stuck sideways in the fish's throat. It's brutal but it works, and it's simple to make. I've seen one in an archaeological museum in Ethiopia and in the hands of a present-day fisherman in the Amazon.

But a gorge is crude; it has limited effectiveness. Its significance, however, is huge, because it marks a conceptual leap. It is the evolutionary stepping-stone to the invention that we all use today: the thing that became known as an angle, because it was bent, or had a corner – what we know now as a hook. The people who first used these things were the first anglers.

To the modern angler, hooks seem so obvious. You can make your own from a bent pin. But if you had the idea in the Stone Age, before the availability of metal, you were a bit like Leonardo da Vinci sketching a helicopter before the invention of the internal combustion engine. A hook has to be fine and strong. What pre-metallic material are you going to make it out of? The oldest known hooks were made 23,000 years ago. They were found in a cave in Okinawa – another isolated island, part of present-day Japan – and were made of snail shell, a naturally curving structure. But it's likely that the first hooks were fashioned from wood, including from thorn bushes, where there's a strong, angled point that's ready-made. Looking elsewhere in nature, inventive fishermen in New Guinea noticed the sharp, curved spines on the legs of certain insects. Native Americans used the talons of hawks. On Easter Island, in the middle of the South Pacific, they used stone and human bones, in the absence of other large mammals. More sophisticated hooks were made by whipping shaped pieces of wood together. A dramatic example is the design used near New Guinea until just a few generations ago, where two sharply acute angles are combined, using a tight whipping of coconut-fiber twine, to form something that prefigures modern circle hooks.

This is the history that is embodied in the small item that defines our pastime. And it's a heritage that it's sometimes good to reflect on, as I did that day on the Luangwa, because it says so much about what is central to angling, and what we should aspire to as anglers. So what is that central something?

Angling, in essence, is about converting something very insignificant (the bait, with negligible or even zero food value, maybe a worm that has been dug up or a few colorful but inedible fibers) into something very substantial: a fish big enough to feed a family. It could even be expressed as a mathematical equation: energy input (measured in calories or joules) + x = energy output. And the magic catalyst x that makes this apparent alchemy possible, this creation of something from nothing, is . . . human inventiveness and ingenuity.

This is something we all have, baked into our DNA and yearning for expression, and it's the part of our nature that should always be engaged when we are on the water, constantly interrogating the particular problem that we are trying to solve. Even when fishing a tried-and-trusted method, in a known place, this part of us should not be dormant and shut away, because no two sets of circumstances are exactly the same. What brings the big fish is an artful blend of drawing on experience and keeping an open, active mind. The secret ingredient is as simple as that.

— 7 —

Less Time Is More

I was on the Rio Tocantins, one of the Amazon's southern tributaries, on a thirty-foot wooden fishing boat that had been hired for the day, and I needed a fish or two for the cameras. Anything would do, as long as it took a couple of hands to hold, as an appetizer for the program's main course, which this time was going to be an electric eel. But I'd not been here before and it was a big river, some 400 yards wide at this point and flowing strongly. So when the boatmen said they'd take us to some good fishing spots, I was happy to go along with this. They duly motored off downstream, and after traveling for well over an hour we pulled in to the bank and moored up. But the current was so strong that I couldn't get my bait, a small piece of cut dead fish, to hold bottom. Only after putting on a lot more weight and casting close to the bank could I get it to stay down. Although it didn't feel very promising, I persevered for an hour or so, but nothing showed any interest.

So they unhitched the boat and took us to a new location, where the result was the same. The boatmen then said I should have brought some shrimps, which started a fevered conversation about where we could get shrimps. But casual eavesdropping had given me some other information. They'd been given their directions by somebody else, and they were struggling to work them out. We were just fishing places at random. It was time to abandon local intelligence and go back to first principles.

I asked them to start heading back upriver. As is normal when traveling against the flow, we kept just a short distance out from the bank, far enough to avoid running aground or hitting any sunken trees but close enough to benefit from the slower current here. After half an hour I found what I was looking for, and asked them to drop the anchor, about forty yards out from the bank. Despite some skepticism, the anchor held, and I waited for the boat to settle. Putting on a fresh piece of bait, I cast it a short distance down the line of the current. After paying out a little line I felt the 3oz lead bump down on the bottom and come to a rest.

The first bite came very quickly, and I swung in a chunky black piranha weighing about a pound. With my fingernail I carefully exposed the lower teeth for the obligatory dental close-up. Then it went back and everybody relaxed. We had a conclusion to our scene. But we still had some time, so I recast.

Mere minutes later, there was something much heavier on the line, dragging the rod-tip to within inches of the surface. Grudgingly it came up in the water and revealed itself as a stingray, two feet across and nearly twenty pounds. Transferring to our small launch, I towed it to the sandy shore, where we could safely get a better look at it. All the way along the top of its tail were vicious looking half-inch spikes. Then, just short of the end, its main weapon: a five-inch spine like a finely serrated dagger. But that wasn't the most striking thing about this fish. Most river stingrays are drab, and blend in with the riverbed. This, coupled with their habit of hunting in extreme shallows, is why they are so feared – because they are so easy to step on. This one was striking in another way: on a background color of deep midnight black swirled a galaxy of yellow suns. It's surely an example of warning coloration, but it also has a hypnotic effect. On the exotic fish market, some spotted rays change hands for thousands of dollars.

This one, of course, went back in the river. But, even so, it was of huge value to us, because we now had a great payoff for our Tocantins sequence. Without any fish, all the footage shot that day would have ended up on the cutting room floor, so the relief was tangible – as was the new appreciation, after the initial doubt, of my fish-finding powers. In my smugness I felt like Sherlock Holmes and Miss Marple rolled into one, even though what I'd done, in this case, was not really detective work. I'd just applied some basic watercraft. But from the perspective of a non-angler I'd performed a trick worthy of a great magician. And like a magician I was reluctant to explain the trick, because once you've seen it, it's obvious . . .

Meanwhile the prime moral of this story is not hard to miss. Fish where the fish are (the right place), not where they aren't (the wrong place). But how do you know where they are? A lot of the time you don't – but you can narrow it down.

Here's a conversation I had a few times when I first started fishing with non-anglers in tow:

DIRECTOR: 'Why aren't you fishing?'

PISCATOR: 'I am fishing.'

Everybody else is ready for action, but I'm just standing

there, looking at the water. I haven't even started to rig a line. Unfortunately this doesn't make for good TV. I try to explain that what I'm doing is vital. But what am I doing exactly?

I know why they're asking: I can feel the urgency. They think I'm wasting time. While I stand there doing nothing, that precious resource is slipping away. I'm up against the popular view of fishing: that it's like playing a slot machine. The more times you pull the handle, the more chance you have of hitting the jackpot. In other words, hurry up and get a line in the water. Having gone to such trouble and expense to come all this way, surely I should be maximizing actual bait-in-water fishing time.

I try to explain that this is one of those yes-and-no things. If everything else is equal, then yes, it makes sense to maximize the rod-hours. But if the bait is not in the right place, then no amount of time is likely to yield a result. Better to spend some of the available time determining the right place to put the bait.

To this end there are three levels of on-site information I am after. The first is actually seeing fish. Sometimes you can't miss them: they jump or break the surface, or they're right there in front of you. But normally you have to look. Looking into water takes practice. The surface acts as a partial mirror, which means a lot of interference from reflected light. So I wear polarizing sunglasses to block the worst of this surface glare. Blocking out the sky from my field of view also helps, either with a hand or a peaked hat. This lets my pupils open up, which allows more light, and hence more information, to reach the light-sensitive cells in my retina. I can now see much more detail in the water. But still, in places, the surface is a psychological barrier. This is because our eyes automatically focus on what is most obvious, which may be surface debris or whatever is reflected in the surface. But it's possible to train our eyes to override this tendency.

One of my many short-term jobs was unloading stuff from delivery trucks for a big auto accessories shop. At the back of the shop, there was a two-way mirror, behind which was the manager's office. This mirror was the old-fashioned type, with vertical strips of clear glass punctuating the silver. Looking at it from the brightly lit shop, customers would see themselves reflected. But if you made your eyes defocus, you would suddenly see into the darker office behind. And once your focus had latched on to something at this deeper level, it was easy to keep it there. (Modern half-silvered mirrors are more difficult. You have to press your face against them and shield your eyes with cupped hands, which is hard to do in a casual, offhand manner.) For looking into water, it's the same thing as in the shop. Make your focus hunt beyond the surface, until you find something like an underwater weed stem to fix your new focal length. Then start looking for fish.

But often you won't see a whole fish. You'll see a partial shape. Commonly this will be a very faint edge, where the dark outline of a fish's back meets the slightly less dark coloration of the water. This difference in tone can be almost non-existent, right on the threshold of what the eye can distinguish. Our eyes, however, are very good at seeing this kind of contrast, but only if the edge is in sharp focus. If our focal plane is too close or too far away, this edge will be blurred. In this case we can be looking right at a fish but not seeing it. There's also the problem, if we're new to this, that we don't know what we're looking for until we see it. So we should check out any anomaly, any discontinuity in the texture of the water, anything that makes us do a double-take. In this way, over time, the more we will see, and the more we will know what to look for, until we are seeing fish that are invisible to less-practiced eyes.

To spot fish in this way it's necessary to scan the water, using the central, most sensitive part of your retina. But while you're doing this, your peripheral vision will be alert for any movement, and you must be ready to go with the natural reflex to look towards anything moving at the edge of your vision. It should also go without saying that fish spotting should be done in a stealthy manner, so as not to scare away or alarm any fish you see, or don't see. Start by looking close in, before looking further away. There have been times, even on well fished waters, when I've crept up on carp just inches from the bank.

The second level of information is signs of fish, created by fish you can't see: tiny ripples, bubbles, twitching weeds, or coloring of the water. Or miniature whirlpools spun from a waving tail. For seeing these in the distance, it's very handy to carry binoculars. And don't forget to listen: a sound can be the thing that alerts you to a jump, a swirl, or a fish taking food from the surface. Hands cupped behind the ears will amplify sound, and I often adopt the practice of jungle hunters, of opening my mouth to give a marginal, but maybe critical, increase in sensitivity.

For even better spotting, I like to get up high. Climbing a tree cuts reflected glare and lets me see deeper down, enabling me to spot things I'd otherwise miss. Once in Alaska I went spotting pike from a float plane. We found some in a weedy bay, and I returned to catch a forty-inch fish nearby.

Then there's reading the water itself, to work out indirectly where the fish might be. I find rivers easier to read than lakes, because the surface tells you what the current is doing. And what the current is doing determines, to a large extent, where the fish will be. To a fish, the current is like a wind, and mostly they prefer not to be in the places where it's blowing a gale. As well as in the obvious slacks, shelter can be found in some surprising places. I remember one place in India, where the Kaveri River funneled into a rocky channel just a few yards wide, where the current was so powerful that it was hard to imagine any fish holding position. Right in the middle of the flow was a roaring eruption of white water, betraying the presence of a submerged rock. I swung in a lightly weighted deadbait upstream of this spot and instead of being swept past by the flow it got sucked down behind the rock, where it was taken straight away by a thirty-eight-pound mahseer. Fish will also lie in small hollows in the riverbed, with the current flowing over their backs, but these places can't be found by reading the surface. This calls for some extrasensory perception, in the form of sonar.

While sonar can be very useful (if you can get out in a boat) for building an accurate picture of depths and locating features such as sandbars and sunken trees (and sometimes fish), it's possible to make some educated guesses just by looking at the river's shape. Deeper water tends to be on the outside of bends, where steeper banks provide a further clue. On forest rivers, these deep margins can be quite snaggy, thanks to erosion undermining trees and causing them to fall in. Fishing on the fringe of these snags can be productive, but tackle should be beefed up accordingly. On some big rivers there are also navigation markers, which help to keep track of where the deeper water is. These markers were very helpful on one Congo tributary that I fished, where the underwater topography was complex and unpredictable. There were places in the middle of the river where, in the dry season, the water was knee deep. Meanwhile the deep-water channel meandered from one side of the river to the other in a way that sometimes seemed to follow no logic. And it changed from year to year, thanks to floodwaters rearranging the sandbars.

Change also happens over a shorter timescale, in rivers of all sizes. Even a small rise or fall in water level can subtly change the shape of the banks, and this will affect the current. If a straight bank acquires a bulge, this will deflect the flow, and this will have a knock-on effect downstream. So it's always good practice to check what the current is doing before casting, rather than assuming that the fish will be in the same place where they were last time. As Heraclitus would have said, if he'd been an angler: you never cast into the same river twice, because it is not the same river. In fact, if you really look, you'll see that the current can change from minute to minute. I remember a pool on the Kali River in India where the quiet water near a large rock on the bank was visited at intervals by a shifting current line, complete with sucking whirlpools. So to get a good feeling of the current-scape that the fish have to deal with, it needs more than just a quick glance at the water.

On lakes it's harder to deduce where the fish might be. But the absence of current makes it easier to spot actual signs of fish – a fin-tip touching the surface, coloring of the water, a fleeting patch of calm amidst ripples – so I spend more time looking for these things. But there are other things that help to narrow down the search. As a rule, unless it is too cold, I like to fish into the wind. Wind creates a circulation of the surface water, and where the wind hits the bank there will be a warm, well oxygenated layer reaching deep beneath the surface. Not only that, the turbulence this creates stirs up sediment on the bottom, which washes small food items into suspension, which in turn brings in the small fish at the bottom of the food chain. Features such as weed beds, islands, sunken trees, sand- and gravel bars and gullies can also attract fish. Again, look at the contours of the banks, and mentally extrapolate. Normally a steep bank means deep water close in, and a gently sloping bank indicates shallow water. But this isn't always reliable: I can think of a couple of places where a sheer rock cliff rose out of a couple of feet of water. So hunches about depth should be checked, either with sonar or by plumbing. Another handy device is a bathyscope, basically a bucket with a clear plastic bottom. Held in the water, this can sometimes enable you to see the contours and nature of the bottom.

In short, whenever I go fishing, I look for clues that will help me build a mental picture of the underwater geography. And a key part of this picture is the water itself: how it moves, and how it varies from place to place in terms of temperature, oxygen content, light intensity and suspended matter. In other words I try to go beyond the mere shape of the water-body, as defined by its container, and visualize the internal, dynamic 'structure' of the water. This may sound obvious, but to most modern humans water is just homogenous 'stuff,' and it requires a mental shift to see it differently. This alternative view of water is perfectly summarized by the sea gypsies of south-east Asia, who navigate long distances on the open ocean without instruments. Water, they say, is not a space but a place.

Having built up a mental picture of the underwater land- and waterscape, based on as much information as I can gather, I'm now able to place a bait strategically, rather than at random. This process, of trying to find the fish or a specific, likely spot or area, is something we should always do before we cast a line. But too often it's skipped, through laziness or complacency. Or – most commonly? – it's the impatience to get a line in the water. In my case, that impatience can come from other people, and because this is a real, audible voice, rather than an internal murmur, it's something I've had to confront and challenge. And what this has done, oddly, is almost make me welcome having limited time. It creates a real sense of urgency and, in a very literal sense – if allowed to – it concentrates the mind. It brings about focus, to an extent that might not otherwise be there. It makes me think, and think hard, before I act – because whenever I've got a line in the water, I always want to feel that I am fishing effectively. It's whenever I don't have that feeling that I'm wasting everyone's time.

Back on the Rio Tocantins, I was looking at the current. As we headed upriver from the unproductive spots, I found a wedge-shaped eddy. What caused it was a slight projection from the bank, which created a diagonal furl in the flow, and an area of slack inside this. Elsewhere it would have been impossible to anchor any distance from the bank, but in the line of broken current we got the anchor to hold, and I swung out a short cast into the line of turbulence. I was reasoning that the fish, like the boat, would find it easier to hold position here; and because anything being carried by the current would naturally tend to settle here, I reckoned they would also be expecting food. Simple.

The analysis of the day is informative. Two hours plus in the wrong places for no fish. Twenty minutes in the right place for two fish. Says it all.

— 8 —

Bad Vibrations

According to Japanese mythology, the earthquakes that devastate parts of the country at seemingly random intervals are the work of a creature known as the *namazu*. It lives deep underground, guarded by the thunder-god Kashima, who restrains it by means of a heavy rock placed on its head. But from time to time, over the centuries, the guardian's attention wanders, allowing the monster to flex its body, with destructive effect. Ancient prints depict the namazu as a giant catfish.

Even in modern Japan, you will see graphics representing the namazu on official posters and signage relating to earthquakes. I had been looking at just such an image – a cartoon catfish face with blue skin, pink lips and extravagant whiskers – mere moments before the floor started to shake.

It was like nothing I'd experienced before. The floor shook from side to side and jackhammered up and down. I dived under the table as furniture fell into the space where I had been standing.

Outside the chaos of this room, all was calm. I was in an earthquake simulator – powered by complex hydraulics and complete with padded railings to stop me falling out of the open space at the front. The cupboards that fell were made of foam. After twenty seconds it stopped, and I carried on with my day. The setting had been for magnitude 7 on the Richter scale, equivalent to the quake that hit the city of Kobe in 1995, killing 6,000 people. But what is the catfish connection?

It started, as many things do, with fishermen's tales. Catfish were seen to become more active in the period immediately before an earthquake, splashing around on the surface of ponds. In the absence of a better explanation, it's easy to see how, following the normal chronology of cause and effect, this might have led to the notion that catfish somehow cause earthquakes. From the perspective of the twenty-first century, however, with our knowledge of geology and plate tectonics, the namazu legend is now seen as mere fancy. But earthquakes continue to threaten Japan, and the catfish connection has intrigued some scientists. To test the old fishermen's observations, Professor Naoki Yada, at Kanagawa Institute of Technology, has set up a simple but very elegant experiment. This comprises just a fish tank, a light beam passing through the water, and a catfish. When I observed it, the catfish was doing what catfish are well known for doing for much of the time: resting on the bottom, doing nothing. But I could see that if it moved into midwater it would break the light beam, and this would register on the counter beside the tank. In a normal twenty-four-hour period, the professor told me, the number on the counter would reach somewhere around 9 or 10. But there would be some days when it might hit 60. And when a graph showing the pattern over time of activity and inactivity was superimposed on the timing of earth tremors, the results bore out the fishermen's observations. On a significant number of occasions, a spike in catfish activity preceded an earth tremor recorded by a seismometer. It was not a perfect correlation, but good enough to be an early warning system of sorts.

So although they don't cause earthquakes, catfish do appear to have an ability to predict them. What exactly they are picking up is not known. One hypothesis is that there are tiny shifts in electrical fields before a tremor, and catfish can sense these. Another possibility is that they are detecting extremely faint vibrations, beyond anything we can sense. For now there is no explanation. But for an angler the message is very clear. It is a reminder that fish senses are very different from ours. While we experience the world mostly through our eyes, through colors and shapes, they live in a world of vibrations, which they detect through the whole body – the lateral line organ down each flank, and, for catfish and the carp family, a swim bladder that doubles as an amplifier. As is well known, the main function of this internal air sac is to control the fish's buoyancy, but it is also a resonating chamber, enclosed by a taut membrane that acts like the skin of a drum. Sound waves in the water make the air in the bladder compress and expand, causing this membrane to vibrate, and these vibrations are transmitted to the inner ear via the minute bones of the Weberian apparatus.

This extra dimension to the senses is hard for us to imagine, but imagine it we must if we are to hunt fish successfully. We need to keep in mind all the time that for a fish a vibration in the water is important information. Decoded by the brain, it may signify prey, or a possible mate. Or it may mean danger.

During the first year I was filming *River Monsters*, there were moments that I wince to recall now – but they may be the reason I was asked to come back and do another year, rather than sliding back into solo fishing oblivion. These were the moments when I had to forcefully impress on my poor equipment-laden entourage the vital importance of stealth:

'What did I say about putting stuff down? If someone plonks a box down *just once* we might as well pack up for the day! We go to all this trouble to get here, but if we clomp around and drop things we're wasting our time!'

This was while we were fishing for alligator gar in Texas, on a stretch of river where they were unusually spooky, probably because of the attentions of bow-fishermen. To underline my point, I once spent half an hour sitting quietly before casting, after arriving at the bank, which probably came across as rather petulant. But it was a point that needed to be made: rushing to start fishing counts for nothing, if the price of the time you've gained is a pool that's empty of fish, or full of scared fish.

I've been told I go into a different mode when I'm fishing, and that's partly a different way of walking. Because it's something I do automatically, I have to stop and think to work out how it's different. Instead of hitting the ground with my heel I gently lower it, by slightly bending my back leg, then I roll my sole into contact with the ground. It's about using the knees as shock absorbers, so my head very slightly dips and rises, rather than the level forward movement of normal walking. But it's not any specialized technique, which needs to be taught; it's basically what we all do as kids when we're creeping up on someone. And that's exactly what I'm doing.

This becomes more obvious when it's combined with a crouch, which is often the case. It's my default way to approach any water – and sometimes, when I'm very close to the bank, it morphs into crawling on my belly. This precaution is based on my understanding of what fish can and can't see above the surface, which is determined, in turn, by the behavior of light when it hits the air-water interface.

As we all know, the surface of water is not a simple window, like a window into a room. Sometimes, when fishing a clear stream, it may seem like it is, but the reality is more complicated. Light passing from water to air, or from air to water, doesn't travel in a straight line. Unless it is hitting the interface at exactly 90 degrees, it bends. And some light doesn't pass through at all; it reflects back.

When light hits the water's surface from above at a shallow angle, most of it doesn't penetrate the water at all but is reflected. If you look at a lake on a windless day, the surface in the distance will be like a mirror, reflecting the trees or whatever else is standing on the far bank. Only if you look at a closer part of the surface, at a steeper angle, will you see through. Something similar, but more dramatic, happens underwater. Any light that hits the underside of the surface at an angle shallower than 41 degrees will be reflected. What this means is that a fish (or a diver) in open water looking up sees a bright, circular window overhead (Snell's window, after the seventeenth-century Dutch mathematician Willebrord Snell), surrounded by a mirror. But this mirror is reflecting the below-surface world, so instead of being bright it will appear as a dark surround – deep blue in the case of open ocean or browny tan in a sandy river. The diameter of Snell's window is always just over twice (2.3 times) the fish's depth. So if the fish is three feet below the surface the window will be roughly seven feet across. At double the depth, the diameter doubles to fourteen feet. This part of the fish's overall field of view can thus be visualized as an inverted cone, which changes in size but never in shape: wherever the fish is in the water column the angle made between the edges of the window and its eye will be the same. The size of this angle is 97.2 degrees.

This is quite a narrow field of view, which would be nothing much to worry about for most angling situations – were it not for the fact that light rays bend, or refract. Refraction allows fish to see around the edges of the window. Above the surface the cone of vision opens out to 180 degrees. But that doesn't mean fish can see everything. Compressing a 180-degree angle of view into 97 degrees gives a distorted image, especially around the edges, an effect like that of a fisheye lens. Think of those hotel-room peepholes. Not only that, the brightness of the image diminishes at the edges because in this zone most of the light hitting the water's surface is reflected, and only a fraction penetrates.

What this means in practice is that if you keep low – in a wedge of space that makes, say, a 20-degree angle with the water – you will keep in this dark edge zone. As you get closer to the water, however, the harder it is to avoid encroaching into the fish's window. This is the time to remember that, unlike us, fish are not primarily concerned with seeing detail. What they register are contrast and movement. So if you are silhouetted against the sky and moving across the horizon, that will get their attention. The thing I do to avoid becoming a silhouette is to keep looking behind me. Taking up position in front of a tree is just as effective a tactic as hiding behind something, as long as clothing doesn't contrast too much with the background. Becoming a visible silhouette, however, is often unavoidable. In this case the important thing is to keep movements slow. If you appear slowly and become part of the landscape, this may not alarm the fish.

All these precautions are most important when the surface is smooth, the water clear, and conditions bright. Ripples and rain make it harder for fish to see what's happening above the surface, particularly around the edges of Snell's window, so we can relax a bit in bad weather. But bad angler-spotting conditions are also bad fish-spotting conditions, so it cuts both ways.

The best confirmation that I've done everything right is the sight of fish close to the bank, acting completely unconcerned. The important thing now is not to get over-excited and blow it. If, as is more likely, I can't see any fish, that doesn't mean I can now move around at will. If the water has a degree of clarity, a fish that's out of sight down deep can easily see me if I become a careless moving silhouette. So it's important to stay in stealth mode for the duration. Otherwise we never know how many fish we scared off or how many potential opportunities we spoiled.

Most experienced anglers know these things, but novice anglers are often so overwhelmed by all the details of equipment and technique that they forget to consider the simple, fundamental fact that fish are wild animals. Acknowledging that fact means setting stealth mode as the automatic default for every visit to the water. Sometimes there's no doubt that it's the thing that makes the difference between catching and not catching.

A few years ago I visited an old pond that used to belong to a monastery. It was exactly the kind of place that used to materialize in my mind when I read the bewitching *Confessions of a Carp Fisher* by 'BB' (Denys Watkins-Pitchford). At one end was a dam, now the home of many venerable trees, whose branches hung low over the water, creating a tunnel of perpetual shade. From here the pond tapered to form a classic long triangle, fringed by reeds and framed by steep banks. Slowly I approached a spot halfway down the lake. It was high summer and the bank was thick with shoulder-high nettles. Normally standing at the water's edge is a guaranteed way of scaring off anything that might have been there, if heavy footfalls haven't already done that. Maybe you'll see a slight flexing of the surface as a deep-lying fish reacts to the intrusion into its window. (Because of refraction, it will appear to the fish that an angler standing on the bank is leaning out right over the water.) But thanks to this cover, I was able to stand mere inches from the water without significantly breaking the horizon. As long as I moved slowly, like a heron, I wouldn't become visible.

Anglers talk a lot about features, or 'structure' – places where the flat, even landscape of the riverbed or lakebed does something different – but a feature that is often overlooked is the margin, unless it's to heave a long cast at it from a boat or from the opposite bank. Fish love margins. It's where small creatures fall in. And when wind blows the surface layer, this is where it doubles around, creating turbulence that stirs up the bottom, uncovering potential snacks. If the drop-off is steep, this in itself is cover for a predatory fish: a prey fish swimming further out will see just dark against dark. But because they are so close to land, even predators will be wary here; they must be approached with extreme care. It's worth taking that care, though. It won't just bring more opportunities; the intensity of contacting a big fish is magnified by extreme proximity.

At Monastery Pool I was in no hurry, despite the slight, contradictory tremor in my hands. I reached into my pocket and flicked a couple of dozen half-inch dog biscuits onto the surface. After a few minutes I threaded my rod through the reeds and lowered my bait, a single dog biscuit glued to the bend of the hook, onto the water. To keep the lightweight bait in position, there was barely a foot of line between rod-tip and hook. My centerpin reel was set to rotate freely. To keep the bait floating naturally, with no line on the surface, and the rod not moving, required a special, energy-intensive kind of stillness.

I was in that zone of expectation. At some point there was a ripple and a free offering disappeared. Then another. The next thing was the pale circle of a carp's lips, underneath my bait. Trying not to shake, I looked into the black porthole of its eye, but it kept coming. Then one of those jump-cut moments after which there was just line sliding down into the water. I gave a slight pause, increased the pressure of my thumb on the spool, flicked the ratchet lever, and the rod transformed into a living thing as the carp surged out into open water. For a few minutes the 8lb line sang as it cut zig-zags in the surface, punctuated by a couple of bulges when I had to hold the fish from lilies and trailing branches. Gradually I edged along to a clear patch of margin and worked line back onto the reel. Then came the magic moment when the rod's sinews relaxed, as I lifted the landing net. Inside was a perfectly scaled common carp the color of old gold, with the long body shape of an ancestral 'wildie.' At nearly two feet long I guessed its weight at seven pounds, by no means a monster by modern standards but a lovely fish for this water.

Such a fish from such a place would have been reward enough, but what made it extra special was the fact that I'd been hiding in plain sight, close enough to look into its eye and almost close enough to touch it. After an approach that had created no earth tremors, and scarcely disrupted the horizon, I had become part of the background. This was, moreover, an especially good example of a day that could have ended differently, if just one crucial factor had been ignored. In this case the alternative story is summarized in just four words:

No stealth no fish.

LAKE

Gear Up

Contrary to what some people might imagine, I really enjoy fishing with light gear. Normally when I travel I pack a tiny two-piece wand in my rod case, just six feet long, which I use with a miniature fixed-spool reel. On this occasion I was using a borrowed outfit, even more delicate than mine, rigged with 6lb line and a small jig.

I was in Canada, and I'd spent the last eleven days fishing for muskellunge (*Esox masquinongy*), the fabled 'fish of ten thousand casts.' As a bit of a diversion, the crew had been keeping a rough estimate of my casts, and they reckoned that by now it had gone well into five figures – but I still hadn't got the fish I wanted. To say I was disconsolate was an understatement. We had run out of time, and the single semi-sizeable fish I had landed, a forty-two-incher, wouldn't really make for a dramatic program. So that was it for muskie; today I was fishing for walleye (*Sander vitreus*), the North

American relative of the European zander (*S. lucioperca*), to give my middling muskie something of a supporting cast at least.

The conditions were not very user-friendly: a stiff wind had raised quite a swell on the lake's exposed surface, causing the boat to tip and drift much more than we would have liked. But I welcomed the increased chance of a fish, and the change of routine. And, to be honest, it would be a bit of a rest.

Unless you're trolling lures behind a boat, fishing for muskie is very demanding physically. It's a day of constant casting: searching multiple locations with different patterns at different depths. But that's not all. Most retrieves are finished with a mini-workout for the lower back known as a 'big circle.' As the lure approaches the boat, the rod-tip is pushed under the water and, without any pause in the retrieve, it leads the lure on an elliptical path just a few feet under the surface for, on average, two or three rotations.

This maneuver is an improvement on the muskie angler's signature (and self-explanatory) 'figure-eight,' but the principle is the same. Muskie have an odd propensity for following lures really closely – sometimes almost touching it with the tip of their snout. If this happens and you swing the lure out of the water at the end of the cast, you've lost your chance. But if you do a big circle, the fish may decide to pounce. It's heart-in-the-mouth stuff, as you strain to see through the surface, while your rod arm is on a hair trigger. So it's also highly demanding mentally: you're waiting for one split second of opportunity, and when that comes you must respond correctly. It's an extreme case of having to be in a state of constant readiness, so much so that your responses must be at the speed of a reflex. And you mustn't switch off, not even for one second. Whenever it looked like my concentration might be drifting, my muskie mentor Don Pursch would mutter his signature words:

'When you least expect it . . .'

Technique must also be flawless. The big circle is an improvement on the figure-eight because a big muskie can't turn as tightly as a smaller one – if the lure turns too sharply there's a risk that the fish can't keep locked on. But for such a theoretically simple technique there are vital details of execution – a lesson I learned the hard way. On my second day a fish came charging after my lure out of a weedy bay, but as the lure approached the boat its great broad head sank from sight. As I worked out later, this wasn't just bad luck; it was because I didn't yet have the technique completely nailed. I hadn't pushed the rod into the water soon enough, and I hadn't pushed it far enough down. So instead of the lure continuing at the same depth, it had angled up, putting the fish on collision course with the boat. That fish has become one of those missed monsters that floats into my head from time to time, one of those recollections that makes me involuntarily screw up my eyes, trying to erase the memory of its loss.

In the remainder of my time there were a handful of other follows, but nothing that looked so purposeful. And nothing took, even when I did everything right. My compensatory fish took in a more conventional way, hitting a spinnerbait early in the retrieve. And that was it. I can remember few times when I've fished so hard for so little return.

The drill for walleye was relaxing in comparison: lower the weighted jig-hook, baited with a dead minnow, until I felt it bump the bottom, then bring it up a fraction and gently twitch it up and down. With the movement of the boat and the lightness of the jig, plus the wind blowing a bow into my line, it took a couple of casts to tune my senses. But quickly I reached the point where I could feel the bump with my fingertip on the line and read the visual information carried in the curvature of the line. (When the jig hit bottom, the curvature increased.) Just knowing that the jig was working correctly, in the right zone, despite the conditions, brought a small glow of satisfaction that was independent of the prospect of any fish.

Then, as I twitched and drifted, my fingertip registered something new. A bite! But the faint throb that answered my strike was there for the merest flicker of time, and I was left wondering if maybe I'd imagined it.

I lowered the jig again, and a few minutes later my arm reacted to another pluck. This time there was no doubt. As I raised the fish from the bottom I could feel a decent weight, which increased as the rod doubled over. Then the weight pulled back, and started running. The spool on my little reel was now spinning, each turn telling me something with increasing insistency – something that was confirmed when the fish showed itself twenty yards away, clearing the surface in a tail-slapping somersault. It was a huge muskie.

The footage of this shows me staying remarkably calm. This is because I had no expectation of landing it. On the soundtrack I'm actually heard to say this, in a matter-of-fact way. That it was still attached after crashing back into the water was a miracle, but this did nothing to give me any confidence. It felt more like a taunt. True, my reflex lowering of the rod had probably helped, to ease up on the tension but not to the point where the line fell slack. But now it was just a question of how long it would be before the line (nylon monofilament the diameter of fine cotton, with no wire anywhere) would touch a tooth, a rock, or the edge of the muskie's gill plate. Any one of these would have the effect of a knife.

But in the meantime we had a spectacle. The little rod hooped over as the fish revealed itself next to the boat, then sounded. Then another moment of improbability, as it came back to the surface. In disbelief I realized it was nearly close enough to net, but a careless swipe would be disastrous. I held my breath as the net was gently lowered beside me, and then – a hallucination surely – the fish was inside. We had it!

The first thing I did was look for the hook. It was nicked through the skin at the trailing edge of the maxilla – the elongated, semi-detached piece of bone than runs along the edge of the muskie's upper jaw. The chances of it lodging in such a safe place were infinitesimal – but even here, a sideswipe of the head with an open mouth would have brought a very different ending.

Just nudging the magic fifty-inch mark, it was one of the most remarkable captures of my life. And it's one that has part of me wanting to point out what can be achieved with a cool head and careful mastery of light gear. But that would be massively underplaying the part played by luck. So it hasn't made me a light-tackle evangelist. If anything, in fact, it underlined the importance of matching tackle to quarry. For heavy fish you need heavy gear.

My idea of what constitutes heavy gear has undergone an interesting progression over the years. I remember stepping up from 3lb line to 7lb when I started long-trotting for chub between the reed beds of the Suffolk Stour. Then there was the move from 8lb to 12lb when I began going for bigger carp in more confined spaces – and even to 15lb when I needed to extract them from the reeds.

When I went after mahseer in South India, I was advised

to spool up with 22lb line. But despite landing a very big fish on this, I soon found that it was pushing my luck in fast, rocky water. By chance I managed to get hold of some 42lb nylon, which turned out to be perfect – both strong and robust – and this became something of a plateau for a while. When I went to Africa, my first goliath tigerfish was brought in on 40lb line.

Then I went to Brazil after arapaima, which meant a chance of hooking something twice, or three times, or maybe even four times the size of the biggest mahseer or goliath tigerfish. By that time braid was available, but mostly in lighter breaking strains. The strongest I could find anywhere was 80lb, so I jumped to using that. As well as accounting for several arapaima, this also brought in a ten-foot black caiman that picked up a deadbait. Even so, I later moved up to 150lb braid for some fishing (yet another doubling of the number, more or less), and this, for now, is as heavy as I go. Although, come to think of it, there was one occasion when I geared up with 200lb mono on a massive Penn multiplier.

This was when I went after bull sharks in Indian River Lagoon, in Florida. Although we took the bait out by kayak, this was fishing from the shore, at pretty long range. In these circumstances there's little you can do if a big fish on the line decides to 'kite' left and right. Even without taking anything off the reel it can sweep the line through an angle of almost 180 degrees, which runs the risk, in this place, of taking it around some big concrete blocks in the water. It was this combination of factors that dictated the use of such heavy nylon line. As it turned out, the bull shark I caught wasn't massive, a six-foot juvenile that had likely spent the previous five or six years in Florida's inland waterways, including in fresh water. But the heavy line was needed for two other fish

I caught, a couple of goliath grouper (*Epinephelus itajara*) both bigger than me. The bigger one was seven feet long and would have weighed around 375 pounds.

Some people may raise their eyebrows at the mention of such heavy gear. Surely, they think, such over-the-top tackle is not really necessary. Well, that depends. In my case, I am not after the general run of fish. And I'm not just gearing up for big fish. I'm gearing up for the biggest fish that I might possibly encounter. And while I admit that such gear might indeed be overkill for lesser specimens, I make no apology for this. I am normally after just one fish, and the aim is to get it in. I don't want to hook it and lose it. My intention is to see it up close and show it to the camera. Any consideration of 'sport' is, for me, of secondary importance.

The idea of sport, in the context of fishing, is an interesting one to unpack. There's a common misconception among non-anglers (and some novice anglers) that you need to use 5lb line to land a five-pound fish, 20lb line for a twenty-pound fish, and so on. But a fish in the water weighs nothing (with the exception of negatively buoyant fish such as sharks, rays, and some catfish). With most species you could support a motionless fish of any size on the slenderest of threads. But weight out of the water is the traditional way to measure and compare the size of fish, and so this is the measure that we continue to adopt.

But a fish's 'weightlessness' doesn't make weight a meaningless measure. It turns out that, from a scientific point of view, even neutrally buoyant fish are not weightless in water. When you lower a fish into the water its weight doesn't disappear; it becomes supported by the water, which is in turn supported by whatever is supporting the water. So when you return a fish to the water, the downward force exerted by the water on the riverbed or lakebed becomes very slightly increased (in the same way that the weight of an aircraft becomes spread over a huge area of the earth's surface once it is no longer supported by its landing gear). This somewhat head-numbing concept can be demonstrated by a simple experiment. If you were to put a tank of water on a set of scales and then add a fish to the water, the weight registered on the scales would increase by the weight of the fish. At this smaller scale the physics makes more sense. And of course if the fish added to the tank were hypothetically suspended from a spring balance, the weight registered by the balance would simultaneously reduce all the way to zero. This latter observation is not so academic. It underlines the fact that most fish cannot break even a light line using their weight alone.

What breaks a fishing line is the force the fish exerts on the line when it swims – or when it jumps from the water and flexes its body, or falls on the line. All other things being equal, a big fish will of course exert more force than a small fish, because it has a bigger motor – in the form of more body and fin surface acting on the water, and more powerful muscles. But the numbers (fish weight versus necessary line strength) still won't be a simple one-to-one match. In a straight pull with no run-up, line with a breaking strain of x pounds can possibly hold out against a fish that weighs $2x$ pounds, or maybe even $3x$. (To an extent it depends on the species, and the individual fish.) But in most cases an angler will avoid a straight pull against a fresh fish, with a locked-down drag, so these ratios are no more than educated guesses.

Whatever these numbers, though, they change significantly when something else comes into play: the angler's skill in knowing when to slacken off tension and when to increase it. On occasion it's possible to tire out and catch very big fish on what seems like improbably light line. A quick search on the internet reveals a 130-pound sailfish caught on 8lb line (a multiplication factor of 16), a 798-pound blue marlin on 30lb line (x23), and a 1,051-pound black marlin on 20lb line (x52). But open, snag-free water and a boat for chasing the fish are not the norm in fresh water. Nevertheless, the same general principle holds, and some impressive catches have been recorded. The US-based International Game Fish Association (IGFA) has 'line-class' records for a number of freshwater species.

Such records are said to celebrate the angler's skill, and that is certainly a factor. But they give no consideration to the part played by luck, the part of the equation that dare not speak its name. Some light-tackle captures are accidental, in the sense that the angler was targeting a smaller species when a bigger one took, but despite this handicap they managed to bring the fish in. My big muskie for example. Other times, though, the handicap is self-imposed. Instead of using gear that's determined by a realistic consideration of what's needed to land the fish, it's chosen with reference to an arbitrary line category. Sometimes using light line is also justified as 'giving the fish a chance,' which on the face of it sounds like an honorable thing to do. But in practice it can mean a number of fish breaking the line. This, no matter how it's dressed up, boils down to losing a fish through avoidable equipment failure, and in my book that should be unacceptable. With too-light gear there's also the risk that any fish that doesn't escape ends up being unnecessarily exhausted.

All-tackle records (such as those administered by the IGFA and the British Record Fish Committee) are a different matter. These are interesting because they give a limited indication of how big a particular species grows. But I'm not sure what line-class records tell us. I can't help but think that they are yet another dreary symptom of our modern obsession with measuring everything, and disregarding all those things that can't be measured.

For example, how do you give an indication of how lucky a capture was? To claim a line-class record, you have to supply comprehensive supporting information, which may include photographs, witness details, sample of leader, certification details of weighing scales, etc. How about also providing the number of fish that broke the line? With this information you could divide the weight of the fish by the total number of fish hooked, and that would in many ways give a more meaningful figure. While I'm in thought-experiment mode, I also like the idea of setting the calorific value of the fish against the calories expended in its capture (including the calorific value of all cash and equipment). I wonder how many of us, including record breakers – perhaps especially record breakers – would avoid coming up with an overall energy deficit.

There's one more thing to be said in the matter of light versus heavy tackle. Much is made of the superior skill required to catch a fish on light tackle, but this assumption doesn't stand up to close scrutiny. While light tackle is a handicap in the matter of *landing* a big fish, it's often far easier to *tempt* a fish on light tackle. And in truth this is probably the main reason why some anglers deliberately fish light, rather than any desire to bag a line-class record. But to this I still say: it is irresponsible to knowingly hook a fish that you have little chance of landing. (If there's one exception to this, let me suggest it's casting poppers for big yellowfin tuna off Ascension Island, in the mid-Atlantic, where you know they are going to get off because you've taken the hooks off. That's what you do if you really want to give them a chance.)

As I mentioned at the start of this, fishing with light gear is a joy. It co-operates with you. In contrast, try casting 80lb mono. Put it on a fixed-spool reel and it just won't work. It will spring off at the slightest opportunity, its corkscrew kinks established for all time. Not just that: even the biggest fixed-spool you can find won't hold the amount of line you need. So you need to put it on a multiplier. But a multiplier that holds a hundred yards of 80lb mono is not designed as a casting tool; it's meant for trolling, or just lowering down to the bottom. So you have to learn how to cast a reel that's not designed for casting, on a rod that's not designed for casting. This was my general-purpose big-fish travel outfit for a number of years.

The revolutionary thing that the invention of supple, low-diameter braided line has done is to make heavy tackle much more user-friendly. So there's much less temptation now to fish over-light for big fish. But you can't always get away with ditching nylon. If you want to catch big fish from rivers that contain rocks, without running the risk of losing that fish of a lifetime, then you need to know how to handle heavy mono.

In short, I'm saying that you shouldn't feel shame for using heavy gear. If that's what you need to extract the biggest fish you are likely to encounter, then you should use it. If I hadn't made this part of my approach, I would have lost a good proportion of the fish that I have caught. It comes down to whether or not you want the fish to have the last laugh.

And although a lot of the fishing I do is off the end of the normal spectrum, the same question should always be asked whenever a line is cast: If I hook the biggest fish that could be in this water in front of me, would I feel confident that this gear I'm using would be up to the job of bringing it in?

If the answer is No, you should scale up.

— 10 —

Have a Plan

There's no point hooking the fish of a lifetime if it becomes the one that got away. Losing a fish through human error is something to be avoided at all costs. As well as making sure your gear is up to the job and 100 percent sound, you should be physically and mentally prepared. This includes going through all the 'what ifs' – all the things that might happen once a big fish is hooked – and having a fully thought-out plan for each eventuality. If you leave it until the fish is on the line, there may not be enough time or mental clarity to deal properly with the situation. That's when you find that trying to squeeze a ten-minute thought process into a couple of high-adrenaline seconds is a sure way to see all your time and effort come to nothing. So don't overlook pre-cast planning; there are times when it can be truly pivotal. In fact, my whole *River Monsters* career very likely wouldn't have happened if this weren't a part of the process that I automatically address.

In India in 2008, I almost didn't make it to the river. From England I'd not been able to get detailed information about the weather in the Himalayan foothills, other than the fact that the monsoon rains were early and heavy. Just how heavy became apparent when I saw the queue of vehicles up ahead. The road had disappeared under a torrent of brown water, too deep for even the big trucks to get through. With nothing else to be done, I settled down to wait.

A couple of hours later I became aware of an engine roaring and a commotion. One of the trucks was going for it. It slewed from side to side on the loose boulders under its wheels, and, aided by a collective holding of breath, staggered up onto dry land. One by one other vehicles took the plunge, until it was our turn. A few tense minutes later, against all earlier expectations, I was continuing my journey.

The river, though, when I got there, was raging and brown. Would it even be possible to present a bait without it being swept away? I was after a goonch catfish (*Bagarius yarelli*, sometimes known as the giant devil catfish), a creature whose broad wedge of a head and massive pectoral fins make it perfectly designed for hugging the bottom in fast water. But even goonch will take the quiet life if it's on offer. And the least crazy water I could see looked to be where the river broadened into a pool, between a wall of rock on one side and a boulder beach on the other.

On the beach side there was a long, elliptical eddy, with the current near the bank running counter to the main flow. But a river is more than surface; it exists in three dimensions. At the entrance to the pool I knew there was a sudden falling-away to deeper water, so beneath the surface rush I reasoned that there must also be some kind of vertical eddy going on. If so, a bait cast diagonally from the boulders into the middle of the flow, with the rod held high to keep as much line clear of the water as possible, and just a moderate amount of weight, might conceivably hold position. I wouldn't know until I tried.

But this was only half the challenge. How would I get a fish out? The combination of big fish and current would be irresistible, even with my nine-foot uptide rod and the big Policansky multiplier, loaded with thick 90lb mono. (Braided line here would have been asking for a cut-off on the sharp-edged rocks down below.)

This is the main 'what if' on a river: a big fish bolting downstream. Sometimes, if your gear is up to it, you can stop the run and slowly get your line back. Other times, though, if you just stand there, you will see the line empty from your reel, until there is a loud crack and it falls slack. This is unacceptable on two counts: you have deservedly lost a fish that you shouldn't have tried to catch in the first place, and the fish is undeservedly left trailing a length of line. Alternatively the fish may stop before you run out of line, but the situation is a stalemate: it has gone around a rock or into a snag, and you are in no position to do anything about it, other than pull for a break. Or you manage to stop the fish, clear of any snags, but the weight of current prevents you from bringing it back upstream.

To avoid these outcomes you need to chase after the fish, and the quicker the better. In some places you can follow along the bank, but in many places you can't, thanks to obstacles such as fallen trees. So you wade along the water margin – but wadeable water has a habit of suddenly turning unwadeable. Or you follow by boat (perhaps you're already fishing from a boat), but you must have things ready so you can cast off quickly. Then you need to maneuver the boat and operate the rod at the same time. There may be places where you can manage both on your own, but if you want to maximize your chances, you'll need a competent and well briefed boatman. In other places, not having someone else control the boat is plain crazy. If your options are 'none of the above,' you're stuck.

And here in India, after traveling more than 4,000 miles to be here, my fish-chasing options looked non-existent. At the downstream end of the boulder beach the bank became impassable. Jagged rock climbed to form a towering cliff; the thought of traversing it, even without a rod, was a joke. Wading was also out of the question, because the water at the side was too deep.

Then I looked again at the river's chaotic skin, and saw a possible answer. It was all about those countercurrents: the deep, invisible one in the middle and the eddy at the side. If I held the fish hard, I could get the current to work in my favor. If I could just hold it from where all the water funneled and surged out of the pool, I could land a big fish without moving from the boulders. But I still had to have a contingency plan – in case that didn't work.

There was one option of last resort. I thought back to some of the times I'd jumped in after a fish. Once was to free a big carp in the middle of the night when the line caught around trailing tree branches. I remembered my clothes clinging and my feet sinking into liquid ooze. Treading water with the rod in one hand and the other hand disentangling the line was borderline reckless, but the carp I extracted turned out to be the biggest one in the lake.

I'd also swum in the Kaveri River a few times, in South India, when fishing for mahseer. As a rule it's not advisable to get into powerful, rocky rivers, but if you do, there are some important things to remember. First, you need to be a competent swimmer, used to swimming in moving water. You need to know that too many clothes will drag you down; anything more than shorts and a T-shirt is a bad idea. (I learned that one at age twelve, when I had to jump in a swimming pool wearing pajamas.) Then there's the thing that everybody should know, if they are ever likely to find themselves tipped into fast water, voluntarily or involuntarily (perhaps having fallen out of a boat). This is: *never put your feet down* – until you have reached quiet, slow water at the side. Floating on your back, ideally wearing a life jacket, with your feet in front of you is best, especially for bouncing off any rocks that might be in the way. But if you try to put your feet down it's all too easy for one of them to find its way into a gap between rocks, or under a wedged branch, whereupon the weight of water will trap it there and fold you under. What's more, this can happen in surprisingly shallow water. Even waist-deep can do it, and in very strong current even a life jacket won't keep one's head above water.

The other thing I'd learned on the Kaveri was the importance of checking out the water downstream, if there was any chance I might end up going in. There I'd not only walked the rocky banks of the rapids; I'd also gone down by coracle, so I knew where the big underwater rocks were, and the slacks where you could pull out of the current. I'd also learned to recognize water that you really shouldn't get in at all.

Looking in front of me now, the water was borderline. Once I committed myself there could be no turning back, and the nearest crawling-out point was on the far bank. So I would have a long one-handed swim ahead. In the current, my course would be an extravagant diagonal, bringing me to the edge of a huge boulder-field on the inside of a bend.

Once here, though, I would be in a good position for rejoining the battle. But if the river swept me past my intended landfall – what then? Would I be tumbled down a waterfall or caught by a deadly 'strainer'? (This is the kayaker's term for the branches of a fallen tree, which catch floating objects then hold them, while the weight of the water pushes them under.) The answer was good news. Yes, there was white water in the distance downstream, but before that, after the bend, there was an eddy and slack water. It looked like I had my contingency plan. It was a little bit crazy, but it wasn't complete insanity.

This, then, is the background to the moment, in the first ever *River Monsters* episode, when I announce, while ripping off my radio-microphone, 'I'm going to have to go for a swim!' Despite appearances to the contrary, it was not a moment of unpremeditated folly, but something I had thought through beforehand – even though I'd hoped it would never come to that.

And it so nearly didn't come to that. Using the turbulence and countercurrents, I managed to keep the fish that I hooked in the main central area of the pool. But then it came up in the water and started to inch towards the funnel. As I shuffled to the end of the boulders, I tried to heave it into a pocket of slack at the base of the rock. It very nearly worked, but then it showed me a huge tail and accelerated away in the flow.

There was no time to hesitate. In the water, with my eyes now just inches above the surface, the distance to the far bank multiplied and the world became a blur of movement. I had a sudden urge to turn back, but behind me now was the current-scoured base of the cliff. This meant – how did I forget this? – I was now in a band of water that was regularly hit by whistling rockfall. So I kicked and pulled, kicked and pulled – a low-in-the-water one-armed side-stroke that appeared to produce no forward component to my movement. Around me the surface was moving crazily in all directions, but I kept going and there came a point, at last, when it became smooth and slow and my knees bumped the bottom. I crawled out and staggered to my feet and tightened down to the weight that was still on the line. As I increased the pressure the fish slowly came towards me, until the line was going almost vertically down, into a deep slack near the bank. At this point, the fish became immovable, nine or ten feet down. This wasn't a snag, but the sheer weight and water-resistance of the fish, broad-headed and negatively buoyant and motionless on the sandy bottom. Even with my heavy gear, there was no way I could lift a goonch this size through the water column.

By this time Alam, one of my guides from the nearby village, was at my side. Twenty-five years previously, I'd experienced a similar stalemate, when a small goonch took a spoon fished on light spinning gear and 11lb line. Eventually I'd landed it 250 yards downstream, thanks in part to the tactic I decided to use now. I asked Alam to pick up a brick-sized boulder and very carefully lob it in the water, a couple of feet to the left of where the fish seemed to be – making sure not to hit the line. A couple of well aimed rocks later, the fish did exactly what I wanted: it swam to the right, up a slope into shallower water.

This was the precise moment when I became aware of someone behind me. All this time, James Bickersteth had been racing to get here with the camera. That was the one thing I hadn't thought about: in the world of documentary film-making, if it didn't happen on camera it didn't happen – and no way was James ever going to get here by water. So he scrambled up a slippery hillside and started running: over a bridge, along a mountainside road, then down a mud path and across the expanse of the boulder field. He arrives and frames up just as Alam reaches down into the opaque water and finds the fish's tail. As he grabs and pulls, a massive head rears above the surface. The thing is as big as me, a nightmare vision of tentacled ugliness. I drop the rod and grab its wing-like pectorals. We have it.

Not all plans are so extreme. Fishing for Nile perch in Uganda, beneath the thundering Murchison Falls, I was casting a lure from a rocky point. Here again, the risk was a hooked fish getting into the main push of current. If it did so, and I did nothing, my 30lb line would not stop a big fish getting to the next point downstream, about seventy yards distant. Once there it could easily go around the corner, behind the rock, and cut the line.

So my plan, if it started heading that way, which it almost certainly would, was to run as quickly as possible along the uneven bank and try to get adjacent to it. From here, I could more effectively pull it off course. It's all about vectors. Pulling the fish's head sideways, rather than just pulling against the direction of travel, is a much more effective way to turn it.

I'd had a small tap on the lure at the end of one cast, but further casts, fanned out methodically in front of me, had provoked no reaction. The director said we needed to move. But something made me throw out 'one last cast.'

With the rod held high I guided the lure towards the place where it had been knocked, a gap between two fingers of rock. The take came just a few feet out, and felt quite gentle, perhaps because the fish was chasing the lure towards me. Even when it turned it felt small. But then there was a sickening plunge, and off it charged downstream.

My plan worked perfectly at first. By running down the bank and pulling from the side, I turned the fish just before the point of no return, bringing it into a big eddy. But then the fish entered the countercurrent and swam fast upstream. I had to run after it, past my original position, and when I got alongside it had reached the base of some white water, where I felt the line grating on sunken rocks. This was when I was glad I'd put a tough fluoro leader on the end of my line. Instead of a sickening falling slack, I felt the fish start to come towards me. Minutes later its huge circular mouth appeared on the surface of a foam-topped slack, and shortly after that my guide Echie and I managed to safely beach it, without ourselves or the fish getting chomped by one of the notorious resident crocs.

It weighed 112 pounds, the biggest Nile perch that I know of to be caught on a lure fished from the shore, in running water.

And, again, what made the difference between a fish on the bank and a monster never seen was something small, and easily overlooked: the small matter of a few minutes' observation and thought before casting.

— 11 —

Poke the Apple

O ne moment to get it right. One chance. There will be such moments for all of us, and this was one of mine. Up ahead of my motorbike are the lights of a car approaching the road from the left. Arriving at the junction it turns slightly away, into a position where it can pull out behind me after I have passed. But, after appearing to wait, it inexplicably accelerates and slides into my lane, on course to broadside me if I don't react. Then it turns sharply across me and I'm flying headfirst through the air.

What happens next is almost automatic, the result of hours of practice. I extend my right arm and tuck my head, and when my fingertips touch the tarmac I roll – along the curved length of my arm, diagonally across my back, and down my left thigh to my knees. After being airborne for 51 feet (I measured it later), my leather jacket is shredded and I'll be walking on sticks for weeks, but my full-face helmet is not even scratched. All I have to do now is crawl as quickly as I can on ripped tendons, and hang on to the car's hood as it tries to drive away. The driver is not yet aware that his front offside wheel is embedded in the engine.

There is also something embedded in me. It has taken many years to see the connection, but what happened that night has, on a few occasions, helped me catch a fish.

The lake had another name, but in our minds (although we didn't say it) it was Last Chance Saloon. We were in Guyana, and a week before, near the village, I'd had a fish of about 110 pounds, but for arapaima that doesn't count as big. It wouldn't make a fitting finale for our program. A few days after that, having relocated upriver, I'd hooked a big one, but the hook had come out after a couple of spectacular thrashes on the surface. Other than that I'd struggled with no result, largely thanks to chocolate-colored water reducing the visibility of my offering.

But this place looked promising. There was more clarity in the water, and it was only a couple of minutes before we saw a fish surfacing – the arapaima's giveaway habit of gently rising to gulp air. I was impatient to start, but first we had to assemble the canoe. This was in a bag on my back: a miracle of engineering that I could have done with in my days of dragging and shouldering wooden boats through the jungle – four miles in one case, to catch my first arapaima. This new canoe was a bit like an elongated, upside-down tent: a thick PVC skin held in shape by a frame of flexible metal tubes. The first time we'd tried to put it up, the frame seemed too big for the skin. Every time we managed to shove one of the reluctant, flexing struts inside, another component came twanging back out. But now our ineptitude was a fading memory: Rovin and I had it ready in twenty minutes.

As we slid onto the water, I glanced back enviously at the crew's alloy skiff, with its forgiving stability and seats that would have made ideal casting platforms. For once they weren't using it, thanks to a raised vantage point on land, where they could follow everything on a long lens – as long as we didn't disappear around the corner. This, in comparison, was like being chopped off at the knees. My bare feet were below the water line, on a yoga mat that I'd taped over the criss-crossing frame, to lessen the chance of the line snagging, and I wobbled from side to side as I tried to get my sea legs. Sticking to this boat was a handicap dictated by continuity, and that was that. But part of me really liked the idea of getting a fish from this thing. I just had to relax and forget the stakes were so high.

But relaxing wasn't an option. The circumstances dictated our plan, and our plan was very simple. Rovin and I agreed that I wouldn't cast at all, unless and until we saw a big fish that we were in a position to cast to. So I stripped fifty feet of fly line off the reel and flaked it neatly on top of the yoga mat, so it would shoot out freely on the first cast . . . and started scanning the water.

In the front of the boat, I held the fly in my left hand, its tail pinched between thumb and forefinger, well clear of the needle-sharp single hook that was partially concealed by its six-inch bundle of trailing bright fibers. Its dominant color was pale green shading into white, with a belly-flash of orange. Finishing off the job were transverse bars of marker-pen black and two staring eyes stuck to a blob of epoxy resin on the hook's shank. Like no insect on earth, this was an impressionistic imitation of a fish known throughout the

Amazon as the *tucunaré*, or peacock bass. Just add the 'fly' to water, give it a twitch, and it kicks into life.

'Over there . . .!' We've both seen it, not far from the edge of the vegetation that tumbles into the water. Then another . . . and a third. Three in a group, and one is big. Their heads gently kiss the surface, a sign that they are in a relaxed mood; then they burp bubbles of used air from their gills as they sink back down. We wait to see where they will appear next, and slowly track them out into open water, as they make a lazy diagonal towards the opposite bank. Rovin is propelling the canoe from behind, heading for an intercept. As well as getting our position right, he's also got to align the boat correctly. I can't shift my feet, so my casting arc is limited: between nine and eleven o' clock. Pointing the boat directly at the target would have me hooking my driver on the back-cast.

A seventy-pound fish surfaces. Its position is a rough extrapolation of the track we've been following, so it's one of our group. I prepare to toss the fly into the air, like a tennis player winding up for a serve. I mentally rehearse my left hand then moving to synchronize with my right, taking hold of the line and hauling it to load the rod, and releasing for the shoot. The next ripple nearly triggers me, but it's the second small one. The next thing I see is a fizz of tiny bubbles, spreading into a circle six feet across.

'Cast!' Rovin hisses. My target is just beyond the bubbles. Adrenaline scours the vessels of my arms as I aerialize the line, push out a false cast (keep steady: it's looking OK) then another (don't rush – poke the apple . . .) and then commit to the final shoot. The big fly sails through the air after the not-too-bad unfolding loop and lands exactly where I wanted.

I let the fly sink for a moment – the fish will still be near the surface – then start to strip it in, my left hand retrieving eighteen inches at a time into the space between my feet, with brief pauses when I trap the line with my right hand and take a new grip. The fly has traveled maybe fifteen feet when I feel something that is almost too small to be felt, like somebody has flicked the line with their fingernail. Beneath the surface, an immense cavity has opened, sucking water and the swimming creature inside.

'Strip!' comes the command from behind me, as I go into a different stripping mode, gripping the line tight and pulling back as far as I can. Feeling nothing, I repeat and feel nothing again. As I struggle to process what's happening I respond to the repeated command, and start to feel a tension, a tension that grows and becomes a weight. But I can't let up; I have to set the hook. I pull nine, ten, a dozen times – it must be coming towards me – until the line is at full stretch and the fish plunges. It's the big one.

At this point I don't have enough hands. Line jumps up from between my feet and runs hot through the fingers of my right hand where they grip the rod handle, while my left hand switches between disciplining the nest of line in the boat (with bits now hanging over the side) and trying to wind it back on the reel. Meanwhile I'm trying, simultaneously, to keep an eye on those loose coils – a snake with the intention of grabbing anything in sight – and the tight line cutting across the surface.

It's a relief when the line is finally tight to the reel. I can now let the drag do its job. The rod also acts as a shock absorber, but I keep it in a flat curve because its lifting power is limited. A couple of times the fish partially lifts itself clear of the water and shakes its head – a violent movement that risks breaking the line or throwing the hook – but each time I ease the tension, and manage to stay connected.

While all this is happening, Rovin is methodically working the paddle. Even a five-pound fish can spin a small canoe all over the place, and it's vital that we keep this monster from getting anywhere near the banks, which are heavily overgrown and snaggy. The only exception is the place where we put in, which is where we'll try to take the fish now, to land it. So our erratic path slowly takes us in that direction, and when the fish's runs have shortened to a few yards, we nose in and I jump ashore.

A couple of minutes later, after some grappling in muddy shallows, we have it in our arms. It's not far off 200 pounds, and our program is in the bag. It's a program that started with tales of people getting rammed by something in the water, and, as I explain to the camera now, the culprit was one of these. The arapaima is a fish that doesn't take kindly to anything coming too close to its nest, a crater-like depression that a breeding pair digs in the lakebed. And although it doesn't have big teeth, the arapaima doesn't muck about. The blow it can deliver with its sculpted, bony head can be devastating. A male fish will sometimes kill a competing male. A big female, on occasion, will kill a male that she deems to be unworthy of her. And once, eleven years ago, an arapaima that was trying to escape from a net set by fishermen rammed me with such force in the chest that I was sent flying. It was less than half the weight of this one, but I was still hurting a month and a half later. So when I get close now, I make sure that my head is never alongside the fish's head. This would be in range of a side-swipe when the body flexes, which happens in a blur. I know a man who had his teeth broken in this way and was nearly knocked out. But if I'm above the fish's head I'm safe – as long as we grip the body securely so it can't roll onto its side.

We also don't want the fish to suffer any long-term effects. So, as always, we don't overdo the fish handling. The shots proceed at the pace of a pit stop, and afterward we support it with its head just under the surface, so it can easily gulp air when it wants. It rests like this for a minute (with one gulp) before swimming off.

Then it's back to business. Bess, our director, wants to get some close-up shots: of the reel, the paddle in the water, my eyes scanning the lake – that kind of thing, so the editor has some options to play with. We can do that just off the bank here. But this isn't what I want to hear: I explain that there are still fish surfacing, further down the lake. From the way they are showing (not a panicky get-back-down-quick splash) I can tell they are not alarmed, so they're catchable. There could be a bigger fish with my name on it.

But, not for the first time on a shoot, I am reminded of our objective in the limited time available: to catch one fish that's 'big enough.' Now we've got that, we have other things to do. For once I can't bear it. Normally I do what I'm told but this time I start begging and wheedling. When this doesn't work, I try a new tack: 'Why don't we do all that stuff, but do it further down the lake with a line in the water? You can all get in the crew boat and we'll raft up together . . .'

To my delight, Bess relents. Then, to no one's delight, it starts raining. Thanks to my holding things up with my grumpy insubordination, it's going to be hard for the editor to get these new shots to cut in. But there's nothing we can do about that, beyond the judicious use of an umbrella, so we set off down the lake.

On the first couple of casts, trying to intercept fish that have just surfaced, nothing happens. But then there comes that almost subliminal flick. My reflexes now warmed up, I haul on the line until I've pulled tight into something immovable. But the answering plunge never comes. I'm hung up on a sunken branch.

Rather than paddle over and go through the performance of trying to get free, we decide to stay put and get some shots done. In fact, having the line attached to something is actually quite handy: maybe we can do a close-up shot of a bent rod . . .

There is a sound like quiet hissing, which turns out to be Rovin, who is trying to attract my attention. Having caught my eye, he nods towards the water, where my line is now making a 90-degree angle with its previous position. The tree is busy relocating itself, traveling steadily up the middle of the lake. I observe blankly for a moment before I make the appropriate response, and tighten down. What follows, after some understandable confusion, is a scaled-up replay of the previous battle, with the early action at long range. Again there are huge boils and breaches at the surface, and heart-in-mouth moments as it turns just short of danger, as the fish slowly tires. The drill at our landing-spot is now familiar, but this fish is less co-operative: there's an extended round of mud-wrestling before we can get a good look at it. Rovin says 250 pounds, and it feels every ounce of that. And we have our close-up shots. Not just hands and line and moments of waiting, but real dramatic action – an embarrassment of visual riches.

At some point in the future, in a windowless room, an editor will expertly splice this new footage with the previous catch. Nobody will notice the strangely intermittent rain. It's an instance of TV sleight of hand that I'm happy to own up to, and something we've done on a few other occasions: implying that I caught a single fish when in reality it was two.

But normally, for the reasons I've given, it really is just one very special fish.

Meanwhile, in a parallel universe, the day went like this. I flopped that first cast short, and nothing happened. I put another cast out, but it was too late: the fish had moved and it was little better than fishing blind. Then I spent the rest of the day not quite getting it right, and finished up empty handed.

Why it didn't end up like that is down to multiple factors combining favorably. Right bait, right place, right time of course – but there are layers of this, plus other details. And where the analysis of a catch gets interesting is in trying to identify the details that were really significant, the ones that were essential for the successful outcome. (This plus this plus this equals no fish. This plus this plus *that* equals fish.)

One interesting detail about my second catch was that it took a one-eyed fly (the other eye had fallen off). I could argue that this made it look vulnerable, and the wily arapaima snuck up on its blind side. Nobody could prove me wrong, because it's never possible to set up a control experiment, where everything is exactly the same apart from that one contested detail. But I'm pretty certain this detail was insignificant. What really counted on this day was the ability to put the fly in the right place at the right moment. And this was all down to something I'd done in the weeks before coming here . . .

We are all victims of pigeon-holing, to some extent, but that's the way our minds work. We like to keep things tidy by compartmentalizing them. But sometimes the right box doesn't exist, and something gets put into a particular box by default. This is what has happened with angling. You could say this is academic, but I would argue that it is unhelpful to think of angling as a sport, because this can affect the way that angling is approached. To my mind, a sport is primarily physical. Its practitioners are fitter, more agile and more coordinated than the general populace. But there's no way anglers compare with footballers or competitive cyclists. And that's OK, because angling is primarily mental. Yes there is a physical side to it, but it's not the main thing – and that, I think, is the point.

Looking at it more personally, I'm not particularly athletic and wouldn't describe myself as any kind of sportsman, but I have always tried to keep myself passably fit and active. I used to plod around a rugby field when I was at school, playing loose-head prop for the first XV, but I stopped doing that as soon as I left school, when it was no longer compulsory. I was also the Gloucestershire schools shot-put champion, but that was because nobody else turned up that day. Basketball was more my thing, despite being only average height (5ft 10½in): my specialty was long shots, from beyond what is now the 3-point line. Apart from that, I've always done a bit of running. And for many years I've intermittently practiced aikido, a non-violent martial art, mostly derived from jiu-jitsu. It was this which saved me from worse damage that night on my motorbike, when my attacker was 4,000 pounds of metal. So I'm a fairly physical person, which is handy, because any angler needs a certain level of physical stamina and coordination. But in some branches of angling, technique is a major component.

I grew up as a bait chucker. The opportunities to fly-fish were far between, but there were a few. As a result I developed a rudimentary ability to get a fly out, and a basic understanding of the mechanics, but I was in no way a good caster. When *River Monsters* came along, most of my fishing was heavy bait fishing, but then some more exotic opportunities presented themselves, including some situations that called for a fly rod. Something had to be done. I watched videos and had a few days' coaching, plus some tuition from guides on location, and I ended up with a passable technique for the camera – just as long as nobody made the mistake of assuming that I was making any kind of instructional program. And it bore fruit. I managed to catch taimen and grayling in Mongolia, dorado in Argentina, carp, bowfin and long-nosed gar in the US, and big tarpon in Nicaragua – from a float tube, no less.

But arapaima were going to be something else. Time would be very limited and I had to catch a fish. What to do? I recalled my brother telling me about a party he'd been to, where he'd got talking to a former fly-casting coach, a Japanese gentleman who had moved to our small town from Paris. It sounded highly unlikely, but I made a couple of phone calls, and that's how I found myself standing in a field with Atsushi Hasegawa.

Atsushi had brought a couple of his rods with him, delicate (three-weight?) wands that he uses on tiny, overgrown rivers. He stood back and scrutinized me as I attempted to reproduce his exquisite aerial calligraphy, and answered my questions about what had brought him halfway around the world to here. He told me that originally he'd worked at the L. L. Bean tackle store in Tokyo, where he would give an hour's casting tuition to every customer who bought a fly rod. From there he'd landed a job at Maison de la Mouche, on Île Saint-Louis in Paris, renowned purveyor of fishing gear to Ernest Hemingway and other notables, where part of his job was giving casting lessons on the Seine. Then he married an English girl and picked up the thread of his previous career in fashion design. His day job now was in design management, for a global footwear brand.

Eventually it was time for the heavy lifting. As I hefted and unzipped the bag containing my 12-weight reel, his eyes widened. 'It's like a Christmas cake!' he exclaimed. Minutes later, despite never having cast with gear this heavy, he was shooting all the line out, into the backing. It was a blistering demonstration of something I knew in theory but had never seen so consummately put into practice: with casting, the key thing is not physical strength – he is not a large man – but getting the rod to do the work. That was the thing that I was struggling with, as I huffed and puffed to get half the distance. Once in a while something went semi-right, and I felt a glimmer of pent-up life in the rod, but I was mostly unable to tell what I was doing right or wrong.

Patiently Atsushi watched, giving me words of guidance, and the OK casts started to come more frequently. Periodically he would make me stop – to rest, to watch, and mentally absorb. During one of these breaks, he said, 'Imagine there's an apple tree behind you . . .'

As I tried to picture it, he continued. 'You are hitting the apple. I want you to think of the end like . . . a spear.' He showed me what he meant. After stopping the back cast it was just a small move, back and a little up – more of a gentle poke than anything else, into the imaginary fruit. It took a while to sink in, but over the course of the next three weeks, as I practiced in a different field, the thought of the apple behind me worked a subtle magic on my casting. The rod was loading more at the end of the back cast. I was feeling, and starting to use, the formidable spring in the carbon fiber, achieving more and more distance for less effort. I was, in the parlance, correcting a problem of 'creep' (anticipating the forward cast) and converting it into the magical refinement known as 'drift.' Then I started working on accuracy. Aim for that leaf, then that one over there. I knew I would never achieve the mastery of a true expert, but I knew enough about the importance of right-first-time casting to know that this was vital work.

It's particularly important in some lure fishing. In recent years I have become a big fan of fishing with a baitcasting outfit: throwing a lure with a short, whippy rod and a small multiplier reel. And the most exciting fishing of this kind, in my experience, is casting topwater lures for peacock bass (the same species that my arapaima fly was mimicking). Often you're working from a drifting boat, trying to cast into holes in the bankside vegetation, which open up just for the few seconds that you are alongside. This means being bold. But if you throw just a little too long you're hung up on a branch, so you've blown that spot. Do this too many times and you end up dropping short, for safety. But this isn't where the fish are: you're now ignoring one of the three fundamentals. Repeatedly casting in the wrong place is hardly a recipe for success.

If you're lucky enough to be doing this kind of fishing regularly, you should eventually reach and maintain a certain level of competence. You might even achieve that zen-like state where you don't think about technique at all: you just look at your target and your lure goes there. But if you only do this kind of fishing intermittently, with long breaks in between, there's a problem. What normally happens, in compliance with one of those lesser-known laws of nature, is that you're just starting to get the hang of it on your last day, just before it's time to pack up and go home. But what a waste of time on the water this is! How many potential opportunities have been missed? Is there any way to avoid this?

The answer is simple and obvious, but frequently not applied. Instead of perfecting technique in a situation where this means missing opportunities, do it in advance of the fishing trip, in a setting where mistakes don't carry any cost. With no pressure on, you can afford to be meticulous, slow and thoughtful. Positive feedback will sharpen your skill, closer and closer to the point where you are capable, almost without thinking, of seizing a once-only opportunity – of making that first cast count.

Hence my daily casting in a field, aiming at leaves, with an imaginary apple tree behind me, before I took off for Guyana.

— 12 —

Thou Shalt Knot

They are the cheapest components of your fishing gear. They cost nothing to make. But made badly they can cost everything.

Fishing knots are very different from those used by climbers and sailors. All knots depend on friction, but the smooth surface of nylon monofilament slips easily against itself. Two lengths of fishing line joined by a reef knot are easily pulled apart. To provide enough friction for the knot to lock, fishing knots normally use multiple turns.

I have no idea how many fishing knots there are, but I do know that it's not necessary to know all of them, or even most of them. This is because there's a very limited number of jobs that you will want a fishing knot to do, and for the main functions there are several alternatives. In the old days, before braided line and fluorocarbon, you could select one knot for each function and stick to it. But different knots work differently with different types, and thicknesses, of line, so nowadays things are a little more complicated.

There are actually just two main things that you need to master: attaching line to a small loop (the eye of a hook or swivel) and joining two pieces of line together. Learn a few different knots for doing these two things, for different materials, and that's pretty much it.

Once in a while, further down the line, you may need to rig something a bit specialized, for which you'll need to learn something new, but your knot collection never needs to be very extensive. It is far better to know how to tie a few knots well than it is to have a vast repertoire.

So how do you pick the best knot for each job? Seeing what other anglers use and recommend is a good place to start. But personal choices vary. Sometimes there's a clear favorite; other times it's harder to make a final choice.

It's vitally important that you have confidence in your knots. With good knots it's amazing how much strain you can put them under without them breaking. But you can only apply near-maximum strain with confidence if you know your knots are good. This confidence comes from using knots that you, personally, have used repeatedly and successfully. The thing is, it takes time to reach this point. Until then you're trusting the experience and the word of others. But there is a shortcut to confidence.

One thing I sometimes do, with a knot I haven't used before, is to test it first in a non-fishing context. With no fish on the line, this gives me the luxury of being able to test the knot to destruction, which can yield very useful and precise information. Rather than pulling against a spring balance (which is not designed to be abused by sudden release of tension), I usually hang a container such as a bucket on the line and add weight until the knot fails. After doing this a few times, it is theoretically possible to calculate knot strength as a percentage of line strength, with good knots giving a figure of 90 percent plus. But these figures may not be completely accurate, because actual line strength can be greater than what it says on the spool.

There's a way to overcome this uncertainty, which gives very good *comparative* results. To do this, tie two identical hooks to either end of a short length of line, using two different knots. One hook then hangs on a fixed bar and the other supports the bucket. At some point as weight is added to the bucket, one knot will fail before the other. Repeat this a few times, varying which hook is up and which is down, and *voilà*: you have an objective measure of which knot is stronger.

This DIY lab stuff is probably a legacy of my background as a science teacher, back in a more carefree and hands-on era when teachers were expected to stab themselves in the finger to obtain blood for pupils to examine under a microscope. I don't do these knot tests so much these days, since most knots in my repertoire are now very well tried and tested; and I don't really recommend that you get involved with crashing buckets and invisibly fast-twanging fishing components unless you're fully kitted out with protective eyewear, steel toecaps and standby paramedic. I include this personal background more to give a full picture of what my knot preferences are based on.

So what are my most trusted fishing knots?

If I were forced to pick just one knot to recommend, it would be the **grinner**, also known as the **uni knot**. This is my normal choice for attaching line to a hook or swivel. It can also be used to attach line to a spool. So just this one knot can cover most fishing needs.

To learn this or any knot, the internet is a great place to go, for videos, diagrams and animations. Just search using the name of the knot and start watching. Some videos are much better than others, and there can be different ways of getting the same result, so it's worth watching a few. Some details of each knot may also vary slightly. Because these internet materials are so easy to access, I'll confine myself here to a few notes and comments to supplement the video instructions.

The number of turns, or wraps, in a grinner will depend on the type and thickness of line. The lighter and more supple the line, the higher the number of turns. Five turns is a good guide for mono, give or take, and eight-plus turns for braid. For braid, you can also pass the line twice through the hook eye or swivel. Or, better still, if you don't mind a bigger knot, tie the knot with a double line. To tighten, pull on the tag end first (the short end of line) to create a loose slip knot, then pull on the main line (known as the standing line) to slide this down. A well tied knot should be fully tightened and shouldn't slip at all under further pressure. Even so, I don't like to trim the tag end too close; I normally leave a short bristle as a precaution. The grinner's one shortcoming is that it doesn't work well with fluorocarbon.

An alternative for tying on hooks etc. is the **half blood knot**, or clinch knot. Before discovering the grinner I used this all the time, for monofilament, and I still use it if I have to knot heavy (80lb) mono. But under heavy load the half blood knot carries a risk of slippage. This can cause it to come undone, or it can result in the wraps strangulating the line running down the middle of the knot. If the line happens to break and comes in with a tapering curly pigtail on the end, strangulation is the cause. An improvement, to guard against slippage, is to add a tuck to the knot (see tucked half blood knot or improved clinch knot). Always wet the knot to help it tighten fully, and check that all the turns have bedded down neatly and evenly. Some anglers use contact adhesive on knots, but this is no substitute for tying the knot properly.

When using a braided line, it's not always easy to tie a good half blood knot. If it hasn't bedded down correctly the wraps can strangulate and weaken the line inside, once put to the test. So always tighten slowly, being sure to make the wraps bed down smoothly. Some anglers swear by a twenty-turn tucked half blood knot, tightened carefully, but on balance I much prefer a grinner for braid. Having said that, I once used a five-turn untucked half blood knot, made with the end of the 90lb braid doubled over, to haul up Greenland shark (*Somniosus microcephalus*) in Trondheim Fjord, Norway. This was attached by a swivel to thirty feet of 300lb nylon rubbing trace (Greenland sharks will often roll up the line, abrading it with their sandpapery skin), which connected to another thirty feet of coated wire cable. Presenting bait on the bottom in tidal flows at such extreme depth (nearly 2,000 feet) would have been impossible with main line that was any thicker. My 400-pounder was actually small as Greenland sharks go; fish of more than 2,000 pounds are possible. With fish this size you have to have faith in your set-up, and in this case the knot was tried and trusted by the skipper and his deck hand, so I was happy to stick with it. In fact if something is used by an experienced guide, that generally counts as a very strong recommendation. It's also the only time I might trust someone else to tie the knot for me.

A very good alternative for tying to an eyed hook or swivel, especially with not-too-heavy mono, is the **palomar**, but I rarely use it because of my confidence in the grinner. The palomar must be closed and tightened very carefully, however. If it isn't, there's a tendency for it not to tighten evenly, leaving a loose loop within the knot. Such a knot will fail long before the properly tied version. But tied properly, the palomar is a very strong knot, thanks largely to the double line gripping the hook eye. It is also very neat and compact.

Another good knot for attaching a hook is the **knotless knot**, or no-knot knot. Because of how this is tied (it's completed by passing the standing line through the eye) it can't be tied to the end of the reel line; it can only be used on the end of a leader. Although this is normally used for carp fishing, with the tag end left long as a ready-made 'hair' for a hair rig, there's no reason it can't be used in other contexts, as long as it's tied with an appropriate line that doesn't loosen or unravel.

And that's it for most normal angling. If you know all four of these you're really well set up.

For some of the fishing I do, there are a few more things on the list:

For attaching multi-strand wire (coated or uncoated) to a hook or swivel I use **double-barrel crimps**, closed with proper crimping pliers. (The pliers should be positioned not quite flush with the end of the crimp but slightly short, by the merest fraction.) These are far superior to ordinary cylindrical crimps; in head-to-head tests the cylindrical versions failed first every time. The crimp should be a comfortable sliding fit on the wire; not too tight and not too loose.

I also use these crimps for heavy (100–175lb) nylon and fluoro, for which they tend to do a better job than knots. First, I make sure the end of the line is cut squarely, rather than at an angle. Then, having fed the line through one barrel of the crimp, through the eye of the hook or swivel, and back through the other barrel of the crimp, I quickly melt the very end of the line with a match or a lighter, then tap it squarely against a hard surface. What I don't want is a blob on the end but something like the outward-tapering head of a nail. I then position this so it's neatly tucked inside the crimp, slide down the loop to the desired size, and reach for the pliers. In this case I don't compress the crimp along its whole length; instead, I stop a little short of each end, to give a slightly flared appearance. In this way there is no hard corner of metal that might damage the line.

These crimps also work well for lighter fluoro. My 112-pound Nile perch from Murchison Falls in Uganda, taken on a lure from the shore, was caught using a 40lb fluoro leader, crimped at one end to a swivel and the other end to a lure clip.

Now for something that I've increasingly needed to do: join a braided main line to a leader or longer-than-rod-length 'top shot' of thick fluorocarbon (or sometimes nylon). By doing this you combine the benefits of both these materials – provided you can join them together effectively.

The knot I use for this, the **FG knot**, is a relatively new one for me, but it has rapidly become a firm favorite. This gives your set-up the abrasion resistance of mono/fluoro where it matters most (the last few yards, where it is most likely to encounter rocks or roots), combined with the thin diameter, suppleness and general user-friendliness of zero-stretch braid. And it does it without any weak point.

Unlike the traditional and more bulky Allbright, which requires the fluoro/mono to be doubled over, the FG knot requires no doubling. For this reason it easily passes through the rod rings and even onto the reel, so your leader can be as long as you like. Not only that, the FG has a knot strength of 100 percent. If you hook an unyielding snag, the line will (eventually) break somewhere else – not at the knot.

The FG knot works on the same principle as a Chinese finger trap. This is a woven cylinder that gets narrower when it is stretched – so the harder you pull the tighter your finger is gripped. In the case of the knot, the more tension it is subjected to, the tighter the wraps of braided line grip the fluoro or mono.

There are a few different ways to arrive at the same result. I prefer to have the braid under tension (putting the rod in a holder is good for this) with the tag end in my mouth, and to build the knot by manipulating the tag end of the fluoro, keeping the turns tight together. Once I've made twenty to thirty turns I pinch the final turns and lock the knot with two half hitches over both fluoro and braid. (My preference is to tie the half hitches in alternate directions: over-under-over-under . . .) Then I pull on both leader and main line to make sure the turns are tight. At this point the braid should darken in color as it tightens.

To finish the knot I tie another four half hitches, continuing the same over-under sequence, then snip off the tag end of the fluoro, close to the knot. Some people leave it there, but I prefer to tie another four half hitches around the braid above the fluoro to create a taper, and to finish with a three-turn locking knot. (You start this like a half hitch, but pass the tag end three times through the loop you have made before tightening.) Don't trim the braid tight to the knot but leave a short tag end.

The first time I tried the FG knot was in the brutal, brain numbing heat of high summer in the tropical north of

Australia in 2015. For a few years I'd been an enthusiastic user of the PR knot, which looks superficially the same and whose 100 percent knot strength I had thoroughly verified, mostly on sunken Amazonian trees, in between catching red-tail catfish. But the PR is a bit of a performance to tie, because it requires the tag end of the braid to be loaded onto a weighted bobbin, which you then twirl around the thicker leader material. The FG is easier to tie when you're out and about, on a tipping boat for instance.

Ashley, our boat skipper and guide, demonstrated the FG-tying technique and I tried to fix it in my mind by doing it a couple of times under supervision. As with any knot, there's a satisfaction in executing it well, and in the aesthetics of the finished product, which reinforces the learning process. And although this was a new knot for me, I instinctively knew I could trust it, and Ashley's endorsement of it, in the severe test that I was hoping to put it to.

I was after a Queensland groper (*Epinephelus lanceolatus*, and what non-Aussies call a grouper) from the jagged terrain around a small rocky outcrop off an uninhabited island in the Gulf of Carpentaria. That meant presenting a bait within sight of the bottom and being ready to hang on for dear life if something bigger than me rose to the temptation, and then tried to get back down among all that sharp-edged underwater architecture.

Normally I don't use livebait, which might seem a bit quaint and anachronistic since we all happily poison fish all the time, by poisoning the water they live in with our industrial and domestic waste products. But there are times when I make an exception and this was one of them. Even so, it was a case of just nicking the hook through the skin in front of the dorsal fin and lowering the fish over the side. The boat's sonar said a depth of sixty feet, so I paid out ten feet less than that, then quickly engaged the drag.

The low point of the next couple of days was a record-breaking on-camera swearathon when a big fish slipped the hook. When it took, I jammed my thumb against the spool for extra braking, but the rotation stripped the protective sticking-plaster I'd applied and started to burn through my skin. To the puzzlement of the crew I pushed through the pain barrier and managed to stop the fish reaching the bottom. It was safely up in the water, but some way off, when the hook pulled. I predicted that could be our last chance, and so it turned out for the rest of that day. But the strength of the FG knot was beyond doubt, and seared into my memory.

The next day was our last one there. On our way out to the fishing spot, we'd planned to do some boat-to-boat filming, but the water was too bumpy. Arriving well ahead of the smaller second boat, we decided to prospect the rocky shore of the main island, in case Plan A was now truly blown. As we rounded a rocky headland we spotted something blue on the shore ahead. As we got closer we saw it was a washed-up cooler box. Someone had just joked that the next thing we'd see would be Tom Hanks running down the beach when, to our amazement, a nearly naked man materialized from a tiny patch of shade and came running down the beach. Blinking in disbelief, we watched as he started getting into the sea, so desperate was he to reach us.

A couple of minutes later, as he chugged huge gulps of water in our boat, it emerged that this real-life castaway had been lost here for two days. He'd moored his boat on the far side of the island, gone for a walk, and not found his way back. At first he'd not panicked. He slept out and collected sea urchins to keep up his fluid intake. But then dehydration and heat exhaustion set in. By day, he couldn't stay out for long in the fierce sunlight, and he couldn't navigate the rocks, mangroves, and croc-inhabited creeks by night. Even so, he thought he'd worked out where he was – but when the sun rose after the second night it was on the opposite horizon to where he was expecting it. By this point he was close to the maximum survival time without water for such conditions, despite being a very tough outdoorsman. If we hadn't shown up, he wouldn't have made it. And if that fish hadn't slipped the hook, we wouldn't have shown up . . .

With our rescued castaway on his way in the second boat to the shelter of our camp, we went fishing. At first everything was quiet as before – but suddenly the bait was seized. Again I hung on for dear life as the rod was wrenched down. Again I managed to stop the fish's dive and this time we pulled the anchor, fired up the engine, and used the boat to tow it away from the outcrop. On the sonar we watched the jagged bottom slowly transition into flat and smooth, and I could afford to ease off a little. But nervous tension was still running high, and it didn't ease until many minutes later, when the fish was finally in my hands, as I stood chest-deep in the water with it, on a small rock shelf at the water's edge. A huge-mouthed beast with spikes running along its dorsal fin like six-inch nails, it was longer than me and would have weighed about 270lb. The FG knot needed no further recommendation. I was just curious about its name and origin. In the case of the PR knot I believe the initials are those of its inventor, and I asked Ashley if it was the same with the FG. He paused for a moment and said, 'I think it's just because it's a very good knot.'

One old and sometimes useful knot, which is also very neat and pleasing to tie, is the **blood knot** (as distinct from the half blood knot). It's for joining two pieces of line of similar diameter, but in practice that need rarely arises. I used it a few times on my early travels, when I wasn't carrying spare line and I was reduced to adding bits of old line as backing. You could also, in theory, use it if a fish takes you through a snag and you have to cut off and rejoin the pieces, but it's rather fiddly. A **double grinner** would be much better, and will also join lines of quite different diameter, as well as joining nylon to braid. Experiment to find the correct number of turns for each line, and see what lies right.

A very simple but useful knot is the **sliding stop knot**. Hold a short piece of line alongside the main line and tie an overhand knot in this, with the working end of this line also passing around the main line. Then make some more turns around both lines by going through the loop a few more times, pull tight, and trim the tag ends no shorter than an eighth of an inch. This knot should be tight enough to stay in place, but with enough give to slide when pushed. It's mainly for fishing with a sliding float, at depths greater than the rod length, and should be used in conjunction with a bead; otherwise the knot will pass through the hole in the float.

One trace material not mentioned so far is single-strand wire. This has the benefits of being thin and tough, but against that it is very stiff and it weakens dramatically if it becomes kinked. It's useful for short traces when lure fishing for toothy fish, and I've also caught large bull sharks on it when using a circle hook. (With the circle hook lodged in the corner of the mouth, the thin wire is kept away from the teeth.) Attachment to the hook or swivel is by a **haywire twist**. With practice this is very neat and effective, and it's a very useful addition to a predator angler's repertoire.

I sometimes use a **Bimini twist** for forming a length of

double line at the end of the main line, to which I attach the leader. The Bimini twist is one of those very rare knots that have 100 percent knot strength. Tested to destruction, the break will occur somewhere else. It's also a forgiving knot; it's strong even if you tie it badly. But of course that's no reason to ever tie it badly.

To make a loop in a double line you can use the **surgeon's loop** (double overhand knot). Simply double the end of the double line and make an overhand knot, then go through again to make a double overhand knot. Knot strength is only in the order of 50–75 percent, so it's OK to use with a double line but not a great choice for single line, where a non-slip loop knot (see below) is much better. An alternative to the surgeon's loop for double line is the **figure-eight** knot.

To join two loops together, the simplest way is an ordinary loop-to-loop connection, which beds down to look like a reef knot. But it's much better to use a **cat's paw**, where you pass the end of the leader through the loop once more, then again as many times as you like, although three may be enough. This increases the surface area of the two lines in contact, and spreads the load. I used this method for connecting my fly line to my backing when fly-fishing for arapaima, where the backing was 90lb braid with an end loop formed by a Bimini twist. The final detail here was feeding the end of the braid through a sleeve of hollow Dacron before tying the Bimini twist, to remove any risk of the thin braid cutting into the Dacron loop on the end of the fly line. For this, and most of my knowledge about how to put together heavy fly-fishing gear, I'm indebted to Daniel Göz, the man who put me onto Nicaraguan tarpon.

Still with heavy fly-fishing, often it's desirable to mount a fly (or a lure) on an open loop, so it swims more naturally. For arapaima I used a **non-slip loop knot**, and on the other end of my 80lb mono leader was a **perfection loop**, for making a quick loop-to-loop connection with the fly line. If this is tied correctly, the tag end should project from the knot at 90 degrees. Don't trim the tag end too short. Meanwhile the loop on the end of the fly line is made by doubling the end of the line and fixing it with two or three small **nail knots**, tied with 12–30lb mono and sealed with epoxy adhesive.

And finally there's one knot for rope. The **highwayman's hitch** is a quick-release knot for mooring your boat. Knowing and tying this knot can on occasion make the difference between landing and losing a fish. I use it if there's any likelihood of having to chase after a fish. What makes it extra handy is that it can be tied one-handed. Just make sure the tag end is long enough for you to reach easily when you've got a bent rod in the other hand.

There may also be occasions when you want to up-anchor quickly. But this takes time, and clearly you don't want to lose the anchor, so you can't just drop the rope. A simple solution is to tie a buoy, such as an empty plastic container, to the anchor rope. You can now cast off and chase the fish and pick up the anchor later. This was key to my capture of a 300-pound white sturgeon (*Acipenser transmontanus*) from the Columbia River in the US Pacific Northwest, which was otherwise set to run out all the line and bust the 40lb backing.

And that's it for knots, apart from a few miscellaneous tips. Don't cut off a knot hard against a swivel, if you plan to use the swivel again. If the scissors scratch the metal of the swivel, this might damage the line of a future knot, and even a small chance of that happening is best avoided. Always inspect your hook to check that the eye is fully closed, and discard it if the gap looks too big. On occasion I've tied a second knot with light line and forced it into this gap, then trimmed it clean. Or close the gap with epoxy adhesive. For cutting braid invest in special braid scissors, because braid will quickly blunt normal scissors, which will lead to messy cuts. Before retying a knot in the main line or leader, first check the line – for several feet in the case of main line. If there are any scuffs, nicks or bad kinks, cut the damaged line off. (With a thick leader some superficial abrasion can be OK.)

Always lubricate a knot before pulling it tight. This helps to ensure that all the turns bed fully down without sticking, so that the finished knot has no internal give, which can cause the knot to fail. Most anglers' lubricant of choice is saliva, although a few more civilized souls use dilute washing-up liquid. Tighten slowly because pulling fast can cause friction, and heat can damage nylon line, or cause the knot to stick before it is properly locked. For knots in heavy mono or fluoro, use a pair of pliers to tighten the tag end. And when tying heavy line to a swivel, a knot puller can be very useful for pulling the knot fully tight. This is a short length of metal with a small blunt hook at one end and a small T-bar at the other, which is much easier to grip strongly than the swivel itself. Finally, always inspect each knot closely after tying. If it's not lying right, do it again.

And with every knot you should practice, practice, practice . . . until it's fully lodged in your mind and your muscle memory. When I was an obsessive carp angler I even used to practice tying knots in the dark, so as not to risk scaring the fish with a light when night fishing. I'd thread the hook by holding it against the faint light of the sky. But maybe that's taking things a bit far.

RIVER

— 13 —

My Life as a Fish

I don't recall ever being so fixated on the bottom-right corner of my dive computer display. Is that an 8 or a 9? Because if it's 19 degrees (Celsius) that's bad. Or it could be. That's the thing with cold-blooded animals: predicting their behavior is not an exact science. Normally if I get it wrong, it's academic: better luck next time. But get it wrong with a Nile crocodile, and there might not be a next time.

I'm in Botswana, in the Okavango River, which famously evaporates before it reaches the sea, ending its course in a swampy delta in the Kalahari desert. We're here to film tiger-fish (*Hydrocynus vittatus*), which roam the delta in packs, like silvery two-foot-long piranhas. Nobody has done it before – it's all about their reptilian neighbors. You just don't get in the water anywhere near Nile crocodiles. But cameraman Brad Bestelink grew up here, and he discovered a few years ago that it can be done – if you follow very strict protocols.

Since the crocs are part of the scenery here, and hence part of our story, we're trying to film them too.

It's the end of what passes for winter in southern Africa. The crocs should still be a bit dozy. But when the water warms up they will become much more active. The switch from one mode to the other happens when water temperature exceeds 18 degrees (64.5 degrees Fahrenheit). Right now, we're right on that threshold, even though the nights are still surprisingly chilly. There have even been moments when the second digit has flickered up a notch. But it's not just diving by numbers: even at 18 degrees a croc can be active, if it has had time to crawl out and sunbathe. So it's wise, in such borderline conditions, to finish diving good and early in the day.

The thing to avoid at all times is being silhouetted above a crocodile. So our dives start with a 'negative entry' (with no air for buoyancy) from our alloy boat, straight down to the bottom in the deepest part of the river, well away from the overgrown banks where the crocs like to lurk. Also, the motor should have scared anything from the put-in point. I am armed with a pointed metal rod about a yard long, but this is mainly to stick in the sandy bottom, to stop the current tumbling me downstream.

For much of the year the visibility is near zero, and diving is out of the question. It's an environment where predators see in the dark, with their super-sensitivity to scent and vibration. But at this stage in the annual cycle the water is like weak tea: everything close is clear, but outside a fifteen-foot radius it suddenly gets dark.

Drifting with the current is a strange experience at first: you find yourself going down a series of steps, but your maximum depth stays the same. It's like being in one of those drawings by M.C. Escher – until you work out what's going on. It's the underwater equivalent of wind-blown sand dunes, with the bottom imperceptibly shallowing before each ridge.

Approaching a drop-off the other day I saw a shape like a log: brown against lighter brown. Five seconds and I'd be on top of it. As my stick ploughed an audible line in the sand, the shape flexed and kicked away to my left, too quickly for my eyes to fix a clear image. Although fish-like in its movement, it was too big to be even the biggest catfish here, and anything but torpid. It was my first croc.

Today we're working along the river's edge, where the flow is much slacker. It's a landscape of thick weed mats, deep shadow, and dark tree roots. A couple of times I've done a wide-eyed double take, but it's just been some trick of the light. What I wasn't expecting was to find it in plain sight – but here it is, still as a statue in a patch of dappled sunlight.

The crocodile's body angles up at 45 degrees, pointing towards the water's edge, with its head just below the surface – perfect for ambushing anything coming to the river for a drink. As per our plan, Brad and I approach from either side, as I try to make sense of my thoughts, to describe the moment. My full-face mask has a microphone hard-wired to a recorder on my back, and I have through-water comms to the surface – but the boat observes strict radio silence because crocs seem to be sensitive to sound from underwater speakers, such as the ones over my ears.

What to say? Fragments of thoughts tumble through my head: the vibration sensors embedded in its armor; the Australian words of wisdom about the croc you *can't* see being the one you've got to worry about (but did they ever see one *this* close?); the crushing power of its jaws, like a truck parking on top of you. Received wisdom says I need facts and figures. But then again – and this is true – sometimes breathless gibberish is the best way to convey the intensity of a moment.

What is certain, as I gently lift the tip of the crocodile's tail, is that somewhere in the back of my mind I am pondering, not for the first time, how exactly it was that I ended up doing this kind of thing for a living . . .

As an angler I spend a lot of time looking at the contours of riverbanks and the current-lines on the surface of water. From this I try to visualize the underwater topography. And from this I try to work out where the fish will be. For this last step it has become a habit to imagine that I am a fish. Where can I station myself so I won't burn energy battling the current? Will this also be a good place to intercept passing food? (Chances are it will be.) Where will I feel safe?

It was my interest in fish that led me to scuba diving, joining the Swindon branch of the British Sub-Aqua Club in 1993. I wanted a deeper insight into what it was like to live and move underwater. But although I had this strong urge to go beneath the surface, I felt ambivalent about it. Rivers and lakes were magical places to me, and part of me didn't want to demystify them. Something about going beneath the surface and actually seeing what was there seemed almost sacrilegious.

But my fears were unfounded. It quickly became clear that anyone wanting to dive in fresh water, as opposed to the sea (other than training dives in flooded quarries, when the sea was too rough), was seen as something of a deviant. Nobody wanted to see 'brown fish in brown water.' So I joined the diving mainstream, took advantage of the excellent training on offer, and spent time bouncing out to wrecks off the south coast in the club's rigid-hulled inflatable.

For many years after that, though, my diving was sporadic.

I was channeling most of my spare time and resources into my expeditions to far-flung rivers. It was writing about these trips that would eventually, through a series of twists and turns, lead to me making TV programs about the inhabitants of those rivers. But because our intention was to pull in an audience of more than just anglers, these were not going to be conventional fishing programs. My fishing rod was just a means to an end: my way of revealing the creatures that elude the makers of conventional natural-history programs, because they live in near-zero visibility.

But if there was any visibility, I wanted if possible to get in the water, and use my angler's knowledge of fish behavior to show these fish in their natural environment. It was an approach that paid immediate dividends. Our very first episode was about the goonch catfish, in the rivers of the Himalayan foothills. And here this 'angler underwater' methodology, using just breath-hold diving gear, brought us the very first underwater footage that anyone had ever obtained of this animal.

Over the next few years I was a breath-holding man-fish in many varied rivers and lakes: in Thailand (looking for giant snakeheads), Fiji (mottled eels), Japan (giant salamanders), Papua New Guinea (introduced Amazonian pacu), Iceland (Arctic char), Canada (muskie) – and Loch Ness (the obvious). Then the moment came when I no longer had to come up for air. We found ourselves with a bigger budget and the opportunity to use scuba. The first time I scuba-dived on camera was in Brazil, when a twenty-foot anaconda brushed my mask with its tongue.

This is how I came to find myself underwater in the Okavango . . . where the crocodile has suddenly moved. Its body has flexed around, affording us a view of its oddly luminous teeth. Then there's a blur and an empty space where something solid used to be, and the next thing is we're looking at its tail, disappearing into the gloom. And I realize that, for the crocodile too, these few moments somehow didn't compute. Just like the anaconda, it probably saw me as some kind of weird fish, but not any kind of fish that it wanted to eat.

It's time to call the boat, which should have been keeping our bubbles in sight. We move back to mid-channel, staying vigilant, then Richard our safety diver makes a partial ascent and briefly extends his croc-stick through the surface as a signal. We hear the whine of the motor getting closer, and before we see the boat's hull we see disembodied faces, peering around the edge of the bright window above us. One by one we rise through the water to merge with the boat's silhouette, then quickly climb aboard.

I pull off my mask as gravity reclaims me. I'm human again.

— 14 —

More Less Is More

Argentina, Río Paraná. I'm here in search of a huge freshwater stingray known as the short-tailed ray (*Potamotrygon brachyura*). But the advance information we had about this place isn't standing up to close scrutiny. The rays are much scarcer than we thought. After three blank days I finally caught one on day four – but at just thirty pounds it hardly qualifies as a monster. We need something much bigger.

Now it's day ten, and I've caught nothing further. It's my last day of fishing, and the level of desperation is unprecedented.

One of the things I keep having to do, when fishing with a film crew, is explain my decisions. Why are you fishing here? Why are you ignoring what that local guy said? Why do you want us all to come back and fish through the night? It can be tiresome but ultimately I welcome it, because it keeps me fishing effectively. These are the questions I should be asking myself – plus a host of others – and I need to have convincing answers.

And in times of desperation, one question that's almost guaranteed to arise in everyone's mind, demanding attention until it has to be vocalized, is: Why don't you put out more lines?

It's just basic arithmetic, isn't it? Two baits doubles your chances. Three baits even better. And so on. If it's all a matter of right bait, right place, right time, this allows you to cover so many more bases. In this case, word reached the crew from somebody claiming to know about these rays that I really should be using six or eight rods, from three boats if necessary. That was where I was going wrong. To which I answered (deep breath) . . . *No!*

Where do I begin? It's largely a matter of focus, and practicalities. If you're fly-fishing or spinning, it's obvious that you can't operate two or three rods simultaneously, unless you're a Hindu deity with multiple arms. When you're bait fishing it seems equally obvious that you *can* use more than one rod – but I would argue that, in most cases, you shouldn't.

For most of my bait fishing I use a single rod. This is partly a legacy of my years of solo traveling, when a vital concern was mobility, and the amount of fishing gear at my disposal was limited to what I could carry on my back, onto trucks, boats and buses, along with a few spare clothes. So it was pretty minimalist. But during that time I learned that this isn't necessarily a handicap. Now I'll fish a single rod by choice, even when I can slip more gear into the pile of film equipment without anybody noticing. This is because, in many situations, one rod is more effective than two.

For a lot of my fishing, I like to hold the rod, even if I might be in for a long wait before anything happens. This helps me focus on how I am presenting the bait. Presentation is another vital part of the fishing equation. Even if you have the right bait in the right place at the right time, you could be heading for failure if your presentation is wrong.

When fishing a deadbait on a rocky riverbed, from time to time I gently lift and drop the rod-tip. I do this to see if I can feel the lead scraping or bumping on the bottom. If I can't feel direct contact with the lead, it could mean the current has wrapped the line around a rock. If a fish investigates the bait now, the bait might not move freely. In some cases this might not matter: the fish will take it anyway. But more likely it will reject the bait – and I will have had no indication that anything has happened. If the fish still decides to take, but the line is snagged, then my chances of landing it are minimal. Hence my concern that my presentation is 'clean.' And if I have serious doubts about this, the remedy is to recast.

In North India in 2005 I desperately needed to catch a goonch catfish for my *Jungle Hooks India* series. I'd previously hooked a very big one but lost it when my 90lb nylon cut on a rock, and after that the pool had gone completely dead. I fished for hours and hours, day and night, at other pools too, without a touch, until our time ran out and we had to go home. Three months later we were back, having sat out the monsoon in the UK. On day one (take two) I cast out again, into a place that had become synonymous with demoralization. I wanted to get the bait close to the rock wall that runs along one side of the pool, without the current sweeping it away, and my cast settled perfectly. Then, as previously, nothing happened. And as time passed, a feeling grew that nothing was going to happen. Although I was reluctant to dislodge the bait from a good and difficult-to-achieve position, I finally gave a gentle pull – and felt nothing other than an increase in tension. A stronger pull: still nothing. Snagged. After managing to work the tackle free, I checked the line for damage and recast. This time a gentle pull brought the distinct feel of lead bumping on rock. Perfect. And with that invisible change in presentation came a profound shift in everything: from mere going through the motions to a state of possibility.

Less than half an hour later a jarring on the line sent my pulse racing. Then a pause, building by the moment to the inevitable run, which I answered. Finally the connection was made, and the fish started little by little to come in. Nobody wanted to touch the fish when it surfaced at our feet, so I thrust the rod at someone and grabbed it by the pectoral fins. Sixty-six pounds of muscle, ugliness, teeth, tentacles . . . and blessed relief.

But if I hadn't recast, I might still be waiting.

Holding the rod gives me other information about what's happening under the water. This information travels up the line, and I read it with the tip of my index finger, which rests lightly on the line above the reel. I'm like a spider at the center of a web, picking up the tiniest signs that something may be about to fall into my trap.

It's surprising what can transmit through the river noise. In 1986 I spent many days fishing a rocky channel on the Kaveri River in South India. Bait was millet flour paste, rolled into fist-sized balls, which were then boiled to make them resistant to small fish – which were sometimes catfish and pink carp weighing a couple of pounds. Even so, these small fish would still peck away at the bait, and I could feel this even with forty to sixty yards of line out, in water that would have swept me away. But these nibbles were reassurance that the bait was still there. I could also imagine the attention of the 'nuisance' fish attracting the hump-back mahseer (*Tor remadevii*) that I was after, which would inhale the entire bait with ease. But if there had been no plucks for a while, it usually signaled that the bait had been broken up, or whittled down to nothing, which would be confirmed when I retrieved. (I would not retrieve too hastily, though, in case the silence had been caused by a bigger fish approaching.) In this way I avoided fishing long periods with a bare hook, which helped me catch a haul of fish from this channel (in five weeks' fishing) that would be unimaginable anywhere in India today: seven mahseer between thirty-eight and sixty-one pounds, plus an armor-plated monster of ninety-two pounds. Hence my faith in the single-rod approach.

But back in Argentina, I'm coming under more and more pressure to justify that belief, to the crew and myself. Yes, multiple rods can cover more places, and multiple bait options. It's standard practice in carp fishing. And it's the same thing when trolling lures behind a boat: it enables you to try different depths and different patterns at the same time. I'm not arguing with any of this. If everything else is equal, or nearly equal, it makes sense to put out more than one line – and there have been times when I have done just that.

But more often, other factors are not equal, and the disadvantages can cancel out any advantage. One risk is that you hook a big fish on one line, and it swims through the other line. If somebody is with you, you get them to quickly bring the other line (or lines) in, before that happens. But what if this other line snags, and you can't quickly free it? Suppose you're fishing from a boat and the fish, meanwhile, is steaming off downriver, and you need to chase after it. What do you do with the snagged line? Who is operating the boat? Can they do two things at once? Whatever you end up doing (chop through the line, losing half a spool of expensive braid?), you have lost focus on the fish, and that loss of focus could mean you also lose the fish. And that may have been your only chance.

You could argue that losing a fish in this way is a case of very bad luck. In fact what has happened is failure to think ahead and ask, 'What if . . .?' In other words it's human error. Or you might have thought it through and concluded that the benefits outweighed any risks. But if you lose a fish having done this, it means you got it wrong.

So, the counter argument goes (in places where they don't have regulations that forbid this), you spread out your rods. You park an extra one up the bank over there, another one over there, and you rig some audible bite alarms or get someone to keep an eye. But now you can't react quickly when you get a take. With some fish, such as alligator gar, this isn't a problem. They move off slowly, in open water, towing the over-depth float, and you can quietly take your time to react. But normally, if you're after a big fish, you have to be right on top of the rod, fishing with proper attention. And if you're not, you'll pay in missed opportunities.

Another big consideration, for the kind of fishing I do, is bait. Baitfish can be a rare commodity, requiring precious time to catch. Suppose you spend an hour catching three small fish. You bait up three lines, and settle back to wait. But there are piranhas in the water. The ones in the Río Paraná are large and golden-colored, and known as *palometa*. If palometa find the bait, the line will start to jump, and each jump is a big mouthful of bait gone. If you notice this, you can quickly retrieve what's left and cast elsewhere. If you don't notice, you've just lost one of your baits, and you're fishing with a bare hook. If you're using three rods, you'll run out of bait in a third of the time, or less, that you'll have fishing with one rod. Personally I'd rather fish one rod effectively for a whole morning than chuck three lines out for just an hour or two.

In other words: just because you apply a multiplication factor to the equation doesn't mean that the overall chance of success is increased. If the effectiveness of each rod is compromised, your chances of a big fish can actually be reduced.

Also, you might not have enough outfits that are appropriate for the fish you are after. So you put out a rod that isn't up to the job. Here in Argentina, under pressure to get a result, this is what I end up doing. I have one outfit in which I have total confidence: a rod with plenty of backbone, rigged with a big multiplier and 150lb braid. And I've put together something else from what I have available: a serviceable multiplier loaded with 80lb mono, and a short 30lb-class boat rod.

I've also decided to do something else differently. Until now I've been concentrating on classic stingray spots: those places out of the main current, where the water turns. Typically these have been at the downstream end of an island, or just below a bulge in the bank. On this stretch of the Paraná there are also small channels that cut across many of the islands. Where these channels debouch into deeper water are also alleged stingray haunts. But none of these places has delivered. Maybe they are the right places, and it's just a matter of time – lots more time. Sometimes, with big, rare fish, that's the way it is. But I don't have lots more time.

A snippet of local intelligence has come my way. Yesterday somebody fishing for dorado (*Salminus brasiliensis*) hooked a stingray, and I've managed to pin down where that happened. It was in a spot very different from those I've been fishing: in a deep, steady push of water alongside the bank of an island. In normal circumstances I wouldn't try for a fish that someone else has lost until it has had time to recover from the experience. The chances are, it's not going to feed for a day or two. But these big stingrays are different. They are so heavy and powerful that on tackle designed for 20lb fish this thing wouldn't even have registered that it was hooked – even with the poor guy in the boat desperately heaving on his line until it broke.

So now I'm anchored up in the flow, and both baits are downstream of the boat: a swamp eel on the big rod, and a knife fish on the other rod, slightly closer. The baits have not been out very long when one of the lines moves. It's the smaller rod. I pick it up and feel a steady pull, followed by another. I tighten and pull back and there's a wrench that rips line from the drag. Then it stops, and it feels as if I'm attempting to lift the entire riverbed. It's clearly a stingray, and a very big one.

José the boatman scrambles to bring in the other line, hauls up the anchor, and then maneuvers so that I'm pulling from directly overhead. Along the edge of the island are several fallen trees, and I'm not sure how far they extend underwater. My big worry is that the fish will take the line into a snag, in which case it will all be over . . .

After half an hour I'm convinced that the line is already snagged, because there has been no movement, and there is no sensation of anything alive on the line. I ask José to drop down-current a few feet then reposition so I'm pulling from the other side of the boat, at a slightly different angle. Again I wind down and lift, but the rod-tip stays where it is. This rod just doesn't have the lifting power I need. All that happens is a tighter and tighter curve, beyond anything it was designed to do, until the drag yelps in protest.

I've set the drag to slip before the 80lb line gets close to breaking point. This gives a safety margin, which I now have to eat into. Locking the spool with my fingers I heave again. The rod bends further and my back sends a message to quit what I am doing to it, but this time there's an answering pulse and I gain some line. But then the rod is wrenched down and everything is immobile as before. The feeling grows that I am never going to see this fish.

Two hours pass. I'm still attached to it, and José's concentration has not wavered, as he continues to hold position in the current, but the situation seems futile. What do we do? Somehow I manage to lift it again, and when I look up I see that we are no longer alongside the snaggy bank; we have come some way downstream. But even though the fish is now unstuck from the bottom, it is clearly a massive animal, and my gear simply isn't strong enough to lift it to the surface – at least, not up through the water column. Unlike most other fish, stingrays are negatively buoyant, so even if they are inert they are a heavy weight on the line. My only chance is to exert a lateral pull and bring it along the bottom into progressively shallower water – which is exactly what's coming up now, where the island tapers to a sandy tail. But if the current sweeps us past, we'll be in a huge expanse of open water, and my chance will be gone.

José angles the boat across the current and the fish is coming with us, an unseen bulk dragging the bottom and catching the flow. The bow scrapes sand and I jump out. Then the sight I never thought I'd see: a huge sandy-colored disc, like an underwater UFO. In the center is a cockpit-like hump, where the spiracles open and close like black eyes. These two holes in the middle of its back are where it takes in clean water for the gills, instead of through its mouth, which is mostly in contact with riverbed sediment. They are also the only place where, donning stab-proof gauntlets, I can get hold of it, to make sure it has fully run aground.

Finally I have the fish I wanted, but it so nearly didn't happen. I nearly never hooked it, and then I nearly never landed it. What lesson has this taught me?

Did using a second rod catch me a fish that I wouldn't have caught otherwise? Or did it nearly cost me a fish that would have found my other bait anyway? What I do know is that, under pressure to get a result, I broke one of my most important rules: I put out a rod that was not strong enough for the biggest fish that I might possibly hook. I should have known better, especially with a stingray. Because with stingrays it's very much about brute force – it's one fish that you can't 'play' on light gear. The fact that it took me and José three hours and fifty minutes to get in is a measure of how close I came to failing. Faced with a similar situation now, I wouldn't put out a second outfit if it were inadequate.

Two equally strong outfits is another question. Fishing down-current off the back of a boat, this may increase the chance of a take, but not to the point where it's doubled. At the same time, though, it reduces the chance of converting a take into a fish landed – maybe not by very much, but any decrease is significant. And if there's only going to be one chance, as is often the case with big fish, then it increases the likelihood of failure. In this way multiple lines can just give an opportunity to mess things up earlier, which is hardly an advantage. More haste less speed. And for me this downside is enough to make me think very carefully about using two or more rods.

In other words, if your thinking follows the logic of conventional, everyday math ($2 \times 1 = 2$), you may think doubling up increases your chance of a fish. But other factors will not be equal; you are introducing handicaps and limitations. So in the strange math of fishing for big fish, increasing the number of lines in the water may actually reduce your chances ($2 \times 1 < 1$).

This is why, in many situations, I prefer to stick to a single rod. And if possible – unless I'm dug in for the night, for example – I prefer to hold the rod, and fish with undivided attention.

— 15 —

When the Right Time Is the Wrong Time

A bad workman blames his tools. Some then compound the excuse by claiming that the questionable equipment was thrust upon them. That's what I found myself doing one afternoon in eastern Nicaragua, in a mangrove-lined creek on the Mosquito Coast, an anomalous region of Central America where, alongside some Spanish, they speak a Creole language based on English.

The tarpon had been on my line for over an hour. In the early minutes it had twice flung itself completely clear of the water, but having failed to throw the fly or crack the leader it had changed tactics. It was now in close, swimming in circles around my inflatable float tube, without seeming to tire at all. My feet, strapped into dive fins, worked furiously under the water as I maneuvered to keep the fish away from the mangroves, but beyond that I wasn't making any impression.

It was a stalemate. I knew what I had to do, but the fish wouldn't let me do it.

What I had to do, and what I kept trying to do, was this. Grip the fly line against the rod handle and pull about ten feet of line off the reel. Then, while the tarpon was circling, quickly pay it that line under reduced tension, so it found itself breaking out of the circle and heading in a straight line, at a tangent. While it was doing this, I would kick my fins as hard as I could, to bring me into a position where I was directly behind the fish, and able to haul straight back against its direction of travel. But I couldn't get my craft to move quickly enough. Every time I tried this trick, the fish would twig and revert to its circling.

The problem was, my float tube was too big. The production team had decided that the normal armchair-style model looked too much like an item of swimming-pool furniture, so we'd gone for what was basically an inflatable canoe with a hole in the floor. But it had twice the bulk and twice the inertia. And now I discovered it had another drawback.

A tarpon is able to gulp air into its swim bladder and extract oxygen from that air using blood vessels inside the bladder. And that's what this one was doing now, at intervals making leisurely glides up to the surface and back down, like a marathon runner downing energy drinks on the move. In the armchair-type float tube, which is open at the front, you see when the tarpon is about to do this and shove the rod-tip under the water, which stops it from reaching the surface. But with high sides all around me I couldn't do this. It got to the point where I didn't know what to do: the fish was so close but its energy seemed inexhaustible. Despite heaving against it with heavy fly line and 175lb leader, on a 12-weight rod in a flat curve, it mocked my attempts to control it. It crossed my mind that if I'd been in a normal boat, with a second pair of hands and a landing net, I'd have it in by now, but that was no consolation. I'd tried fishing from a boat, and it doesn't work here. This fish would have spooked and wouldn't have taken the fly. It was the giant duck-man approach or nothing.

But as an angler tires, so too does the fish. For the umpteenth time I spun and kicked, and this time the tarpon was too slow to react, and I brought it to a grudging halt. With its momentum gone, it had to summon energy from its reserves to restart. It was a palpable shift in the balance of power. I had overcome the handicap of my too-heavy vessel, but my energy was also getting low. We were like a couple of boxers on the ropes, but I could now see a way to an outcome in my favor. A few more successful spin-and-kick maneuvers and I was getting close to the point where I could maybe grab the leader. But this end game, the time of getting hands on the fish, is also the time when any error is most likely to be punished.

It's a time for judgment, technique, speed and surprise. First, you have to get the fish to within a few feet, and pick a moment to act. What you have to do is lift the rod-tip from its low position close to the water into a position above you or even extended slightly behind, to bring the line in close enough to reach. With such a flexible rod, you can only do this by paying line out from the reel and easing the pressure on the fish. As with the anti-circling maneuver, the line-release has to be done in two stages: with the 'live' line trapped against the rod handle pull a long loop of slack from the reel, then quickly release this slack while raising the rod. With the rod vertical, you are now 'high sticking,' something which in normal circumstances is not recommended. There is a dangerously acute angle between rod and line. If the fish takes off now you must drop the rod-tip immediately; otherwise it will snap. If the fish is still where you want it, however, you extend your free hand and grasp the leader. But there's a right way and a wrong way to do this.

In order to get a grip on the thin, smooth line, it's necessary to wrap it once or twice around your hand. But if you do this unthinkingly and make the wraps from the line above your hand, and the fish decides to bolt, you could be in trouble. Even if you open your hand, the line can tighten around it, rather than spilling off. If this happens, you could end up in the water attached to a fish that weighs well over a hundred pounds, which is potentially a very dangerous scenario if you can't release yourself. If you've ever tried to break 175lb line with your hands you know that this isn't possible . . .

The important thing, therefore, is to make any wraps going down the leader, so at any moment you can open your hand and allow the line to spill off – 'dumping the line' in the parlance of the deck hands who (wearing gloves) bring in sharks and 1,000-pound marlin this way. It's another of those crucial things that you need to think about and plan before fishing, so it happens automatically, rather than taking up valuable head space when there are other things to think about and react to. But more than that, it's something that needs to be rehearsed. Your arm needs to know what it feels like to make the correct move, and your hand needs to know how it feels to take the line in the correct way. It sounds paradoxical, but you need muscle memory already in place before you do this on a fish for the first time. But this is possible. You can tie a few feet of line to a bag and work with that. Then, taking a tip from dancers and gymnasts, athletes and musicians, surgeons and martial artists, you can keep it fresh by visualizing the procedure in your mind. You can also mime the movements, which looks like a cross between a t'ai chi routine and a game of charades. Ultimately, the more familiar you are with what you have to do, the less likely you are to fumble when the time comes.

Lining a tarpon from a float tube is an extreme case of a drill that has to be followed correctly. But there are simpler, more everyday things that benefit from actual and/or mental rehearsal, like finding your reel drag in a hurry, maybe in the dark. Or operating a landing net when fishing solo.

With most fish you'll grab the leader once and that will be it. But on this day things weren't that simple. On the first attempt, the tarpon kicked and started towing me and I had to dump the line. The stamina of this fish was unbelievable, but this escalation was making it tire. Even so, I had to make a few more grabs before, finally, I didn't have to let go. The tarpon was on the surface beside me and I could see the fly, hooked in the edge of its mouth. To get to this point had taken two hours.

Lightly holding the now-still fish I removed the fly, then prepared to show my catch to the camera by pulling its front end briefly out of the water. I went to grip its jaw by putting both thumbs in its mouth, which works well if you're in an armchair-type float tube, where you can get the fish in front of you. But it felt awkward: I was having to twist to my left and work over the top of an inflated tube. This, combined with the way the fish was now lying, with its body hanging down in the water, meant that I should have tried for a different grip, with my fingers gripping the inside of the lower jaw and my thumbs outside. But that's me talking with hindsight. At the time I tried to press ahead with Plan A, despite it feeling wrong. And while I was doing this, the fish gave one final kick, twisted out of my grip, and was gone.

The expression on the director's face was the biggest grin you could imagine. From the perspective of a dramatist, the unfakeable emotion that follows such an epic loss is pure TV gold. It also sets up the final success as being so much more significant – if there is final success. From an angler's point of view, though, losing a fish through human error is unacceptable. The only thing that redeems it is the learning of a lesson, to make sure the error never happens again.

With this fish I did everything right until the very last moment. Then, partly through fatigue, I lost concentration. And that's all it takes.

Some kind souls have pointed out that, in certain circles, touching the leader counts as a capture. But I wanted to get a clear look at the fish, and in that I failed. In need of solace, though, I also remembered what went right. The stamina of that fish was, and still is, hard to believe. But despite the handicap of my heavy craft, I managed, eventually, to out-maneuver it and start wearing it down. Then there was the precarious procedure of manipulating the rod and taking hold of the leader, which each time happened without disaster. If I'd not planned and rehearsed, I wouldn't have got this fish as close as I did; and in light of this I found myself feeling confident for the next encounter – if there was one. But I was not going to fish anymore that day. To come back physically sharp and clear headed, I needed some recovery time . . .

Sometimes, as it was with these tarpon, it really is like training for a fight. Your opponent has strengths and weaknesses, and to counter their moves you need moves of your own. But it's not enough just to plan them; you need to be able to execute them, flawlessly and without hesitation. Any lack of preparedness will be punished, and the outcome won't be in your favor. The fact that the fish takes your bait will be an irrelevance, because being unprepared turns the right time into the wrong time. In short, treating an opportunity to catch a big fish as if it were a rehearsal is asking for failure. Don't even put the bait in the water unless you're confident of getting the fish in.

The next day I was back on the water, on a large, mirror-like lagoon, inching a shrimp imitation through what appeared to be a tarpon corridor. Eventually, after a series of methodical casts, some better executed than others, fly and tarpon coincided, signaled by a metallic flick on the line. This time all my reflexes were more flowing and confident, and after bringing the fish in, I secured it properly, then released it.

I finished my time on the Mosquito Coast with two big tarpon – one of them a good 150 pounds – and a renewed appreciation of the importance of rehearsal.

— 16 —

Mumbo-Jumbo

In advertising, so the famous saying goes, half the money you spend is wasted. But you never know which half. In angling too, sometimes it's impossible to say what was significant and what was not . . .

Many years ago, having decided it might be time to blend in more with my peers, I made a visit to London's Oxford Street. I quickly found what I was looking for: a shop devoted entirely to clothes made from denim. Behind the counter, clad in the products of his emporium, lounged a man with long golden curly hair. He was surrounded by a group of young women, in postures of casual adoration and similar attire, who may have been customers or staff, but who, either way, weren't more than momentarily interested in my non-denim-clad presence. Overwhelmed by such a cornucopia of clothing, I started to flick through the nearest rack, pretending to appraise the material and stitch quality, but in fact afflicted by an attack of retail paralysis. Given time, though, I was confident that I would find something I liked.

At least I was, until the manager spoke. 'Those are for chicks, man.'

Recalling them now, I laugh at his drawled words, but at the time they brought a hot glow to my face, as I slunk from the shop without even trying on a waistcoat.

Some years later, in 1986, I was just days away from traveling to India, to fish for mahseer, but I hadn't found anything close to the rod I needed. In quantitative terms I wanted something about ten feet long, with a good through-action, and a test curve of about four pounds, twice the backbone of my most muscular carp rod, but there was no off-the-peg solution. In desperation I reckoned I could get an eleven-foot pike rod, chop six inches off the tip and butt, and that would be more or less what I wanted. So I went into one of my local tackle shops, in search of a suitable subject for butchery.

It was a similar configuration: man behind counter, surrounded by lounging mates. When I described what I was looking for and why, I was, quite literally, laughed out of the shop. My mention of a four-pound test curve brought popping eyes and spluttered exclamations: 'Never heard of it!'

Luckily I was saved by a more understanding fellow, a well-known fishing-tackle magnate from the Midlands, who had just what I wanted – almost. It was an eleven-foot surfcasting rod, built from two equal-length pieces of brown hollow fiberglass, and designed for bass. When I got it home I took off the rings and respaced them (adding one more) so that when I matched it with my chosen reel (an Abu Ambassadeur 7000 multiplier) and clamped the butt horizontally in a vise, I could hang a four-pound weight on the line without it touching the rod between the guides at any point. Then I hacksawed six inches off the butt and it was ready to go.

When I brought it home from India, nearly six months later, there were grooves burnt by running line in the plastic grip above the reel mount, but otherwise it was intact. More than that, it had brought in mahseer to ninety-two pounds. At the time, I couldn't imagine a tougher test for a rod. So when I went to the Congo four years later, after goliath tigerfish, I took it with me – despite it being a bit on the long side for boat fishing (even after taking a bit more off the butt) and despite having the loan of something more high-tech and purpose-built. That two-month trip was a blank, but on the rematch the next year, when the chosen tributary wasn't in flood, the same rod brought my first goliath, a fish of 38½ pounds – a creature that most people hadn't even heard of at the time.

At this point this plain-looking tool became, unofficially, my lucky rod. This was partly to do with its mechanical capabilities, but it was more than that. Sometimes an object becomes imbued with significance, a strange power. When you take it in your hands it completes a circuit. An identical replacement wouldn't be the same. It has something, which, like a soul, can't be weighed. Because you've come through testing moments together, it becomes part of you. Or so it feels. And so I took it to the Amazon, when I went looking for arapaima, a fish that potentially dwarfs the other creatures it had handled.

By this time, technically better options were available. Carbon fiber (graphite) was becoming more affordable and quickly replacing hollow fiberglass, so my mahseer rod was now something of an old-fashioned relic. But although slightly heavier than carbon, glass was tried and tested, and known to be robust. And for the kind of fishing I was doing the difference in weight was academic. The main problem was safely transporting it. With its unequal two-piece configuration, where the more delicate tip was the longer piece, it was not ideal. But with careful packing in a piece of drainpipe the right size, this difficulty was overcome.

To cut a very long story short, this rod, having already brought me mahseer and goliath tigerfish, went on to catch several arapaima. In doing so it became the only rod in existence to have caught these three iconic freshwater species, reason enough to consider it something special. A few years later I retired it, which felt like giving an old friend a well-earned rest. In the end, this wasn't too hard a decision. For a start it was time to scale up a bit. And by now there were some off-the-peg rods that better suited my needs.

For the most part though I was still improvising, making creative (read 'incorrect') use of saltwater gear. For example, when I returned to India to target goonch catfish I used nine-foot uptide rods, which worked really well, apart from not being designed to travel, thanks to having two very unequal sections. I also started to acquire some rods that were purpose-built; a couple I built myself, and I've been given a few too. Over time, thanks to the lucky situation I find myself in, I've also accumulated quite a collection of specialist tools: a popping rod for giant trevally, heavy fly rods, a rod for shore-based shark fishing . . .

In some respects it's now a far cry from the solo fishing that I used to do, but I still have a few heavy bait-fishing rods that I use for maybe half of my fishing. A couple of these are designed for big wels catfish and there's an even heavier rod that I had built to my specs. None of these, though, has achieved the same significance as that mahseer rod. Perhaps that's because my fishing back then used to be more self-reliant. During a two- or three-month trip, most of the time would be consumed by traveling – by riverboat, truck or bus – or waiting for transport that hardly ever came. On one Amazon riverboat we were packed so tight that I could have reached out from my hammock and touched thirteen other passengers. It's not often you can say that about your sleeping quarters. Two or three nights into this voyage I was woken by an impact and a lurch. People were screaming and running to the rails. The chain to the tiller had broken and we'd rammed the bank. Luckily we didn't tip and sink. On another occasion, though, I was asleep on a boat which did sink, and got out with just seconds to spare.

On these earlier trips I was in a different head space, often exhausted, sleep-deprived and frustrated, and having to deal with all this on my own. In such circumstances, when your world is reduced to what you can carry, you become very attached to those few objects. And in this context, a fiberglass fishing rod stands out as something rather preposterous, because despite having its special hidden strength it is a thing of great fragility. It needs looking after and protecting. There's an investment of care that seems out of place towards something inanimate.

But here's something strange that this inanimate object did. When beset by the feeling that I often have, that capturing a particular fish is near-impossible, it was a tangible reminder that I'd prevailed in such circumstances before. It bestowed a degree of confidence, which is always a valuable commodity when fishing, because it boosts attention. So my reference to my old mahseer rod as my lucky rod is not entirely tongue-in-cheek. There is some basis to looking at it this way, which does stand up to scrutiny.

But a rod is a functional part of the machinery that catches a fish. What's the deal with something like a lucky hat or a lucky ritual, such as making a cup of tea from lake water on arrival? Fishermen have always been well known for their superstitions, especially when fishing at sea. Whistling on a boat is said to be unlucky, because it summons high winds and rough weather, but I've never heard a skipper admonish anyone on this matter. But I have come across a number of skippers who won't allow bananas on their boat, because they believe it brings bad luck. Very few can tell you where this belief came from. Maybe it's because in the old days a cargo of bananas might harbor stowaways in the form of venomous creepy-crawlies or snakes. More likely it's because bananas hasten the ripening of other fruit, so on a long voyage they could cause citrus fruits such as limes to go 'off,' and hence make passengers and crew vulnerable to scurvy. It seems to be in that category of beliefs that used to have a good reason behind it, but it hardly applies on a day out in a motor launch. Even so, if somebody in the film crew has inadvertently packed bananas with our lunch, I'm right there with the boat crew if they request we leave them ashore. I believe that our observance or non-observance might affect our prospects, because it changes the atmosphere and expectations.

This opens out into a wider consideration of respecting beliefs. A lot of my catches are down to collaboration with local fishermen, and in some places my visit has included a visit to a shaman or witch doctor. Inevitably somebody will watch this and be moved to tick me off for giving airtime to what they see as heathen mumbo-jumbo. My reaction, when this happens, is unapologetic. OK, part of the reason is to add a bit of color, but it's not gratuitous. If my local collaborator believes that my being blessed or protected or whatever increases our chances, then that makes it worth doing, for the same reason that I don't take bananas on boats if asked not to. But it goes beyond that.

It's also being respectful to beliefs that deserve respect. While some beliefs that some people hold deserve to be challenged, a lot of so-called primitive beliefs don't fall into that category, and here's why. Most rituals to ensure a fisherman's safety or good fortune entail making some kind of offering to the water, or to the water's guardian spirits. In Mongolia I visited a shaman who was, unusually, a young woman. Robed in long strips of bright-colored cloth and an elaborate blindfold, she whirled like a dervish and beat a drum of animal hide, and when she next spoke her voice had transformed to a harsh old-man's croak. She told me that before I fished I should make an offering to the river spirit, who was the guardian of the fish. Specifically, I should take a bowl of yak's milk and flick some of it towards the river and some on the riverbank.

From a scientific viewpoint, there is no mechanism whereby this can influence the outcome of a day's fishing. Or is there? It's interesting that the idea of making a symbolic offering to the water is widespread across so many different cultures. Often tied in with this is the belief that you shouldn't take more than you need, and that if you do you are liable to be punished. In the tidal swamps of the Sundarbans, at the mouth of the Ganges, the goddess Banbibi will protect you from man-eating tigers – but only if you just take what you need, and no more. On the Zambezi the Nyami-nyami spirit protects fishermen, but is vengeful if the river is harmed. In the Amazon the *mãe d'água*, the mother of the water, is likewise not to be provoked by over-exploitation. Such views are of course characterized as primitive, but a moment's thought will reveal a simple wisdom that our supposedly more developed culture has forgotten. Therefore, when I remember, I do what the Mongolian shaman told me. I don't have the yak's milk anymore, but I try to take a moment to reflect on our relationship with the water and with the fish. They are a gift, whose presence is not to be taken for granted, and our fishing should be a respectful act. This won't necessarily help us catch more fish today – but it does have the potential to help others catch fish in the future. And it makes those we catch today more significant and more deserved.

Meanwhile if you want to wear your lucky hat, even if it's from that denim shop on Oxford Street, you will hear no mockery from me.

DELTA

— 17 —

Resist the Flow

At a certain popular lake in south-east England, the far bank was a no-fishing zone, so the standard method was to belt out baits towards the opposite margin, some eighty yards away. The lake didn't produce a lot of fish, but the thinking behind this approach was vindicated by the fact that most captures came from this area.

I arrived one evening in a feverish state of mind. It was high summer, and on the four-hour journey from the other side of the country my old Mini had been constantly on the verge of boiling over. The only way to keep it going had been to run it all the way with the heater on full blast. Maybe this was why I decided, after my customary few minutes of sitting and thinking, to try something different.

Although there was always a fair amount of foot-clomping on the near bank – why be stealthy if your baits are nowhere near? – I reasoned that the fish might feel quite safe in the near margins, at least in the small, dark hours of the morning. This was because, I hypothesized, no fish ever got caught from here. And that was because nobody ever put a bait here. My chosen spot was opposite the end of a wooded peninsula that almost divided the lake into two, and my plan was to drop my freelined bait just short of this. I waited until nobody was watching and made a gentle under-arm swing.

Besides my non-macho casting, there was another reason my cautious optimism was tinged with embarrassment. On my hook was something that no self-respecting carp angler had used for years: a boiled potato. But I had been thinking lately about the current fashion for high-protein baits – gourmet concoctions that would have made even the most pampered household pet green with envy – and, again, I wanted to try something different. This was not just for the sake of being perverse, but based on the principles of nutrition. While there was no doubt that the new HP baits were very successful, I was not sure it was all about protein content.

'Protein good, carbohydrate bad' is the boiled-down message of most food advertising, so that's what most people believe. But our need for energy is much greater than our need for the raw materials for growth and repair. Having said that, most people in the developed world take in way more carbs than they need, without even trying. Just look at the labeling on processed food, if you've got a magnifying glass handy, and you will see sugar hidden everywhere, from chocolate to mayonnaise, breakfast cereals to baked beans. So humans are indeed well advised to cut down on their intake.

But if you're a wild animal, you'll take all the carbs you can get. So much so that if you're short, you'll feed the precious amino acids that are yielded from the digestion of proteins into the energy-release pathway. For day-to-day survival, protein is a luxury, but carbohydrate is a necessity. So carp will be anything but carb-averse. Hence my choice of a potato, with a few loose offerings scattered around to get their attention – although I'd not gone the whole hog and done any kind of prebaiting.

I also factored in a regard for a carp's curiosity. I was offering something new, which had no negative associations.

The darkness grew thicker, and the world became quiet. Lying on my bed-chair, I entered that state of vigilant relaxation where the stillness has the feel of a frozen moment. Just the occasional cough, or a hint of a murmur rolling across the water, betrayed the passage of time. Then, induced by just the right frequency of alert inattentiveness, came the low buzz from my bite alarm. Without being aware of exactly how I got there, I was standing at the water's edge, holding a rod that was now connected to something alive. After a brief but intense tussle, in that grey territory where the outcome is ninety-odd parts determined by human competence and assiduousness, and the unknown remainder in the lap of the gods, a carp was in the landing net. I parted the meshes to reveal the net-like pattern of a fully scaled flank – the rare sight of a 'common' carp, a variety which in this lake and most others is now outnumbered by its partially scaled brethren. At nine pounds it wasn't a big one, for this water where the hope was always for a fish over twenty, but on a night that was otherwise quiet it was ample in terms of satisfaction.

This was the simple pleasure that comes from doing something new and different, and being rewarded with a result. This occasional deviation from the norm, rather than always sticking to an established repertoire, can be seen as a behavioral mutation: it's something which might lead nowhere but which on the odd occasion might lead somewhere interesting or even revolutionary. It's the way one evolves as an angler. But if you keep doing what you always do, you'll keep getting what you always get.

Probably the best example of an angling mutation that turned out to be revolutionary was the development of the hair rig in the late 1970s. Prior to this, who would have thought that fishing a bare hook, with the bait dangling underneath it, would be any use as a technique? Like many of the best inventions it was, on the face of it, counterintuitive. But once it existed, and its effectiveness had been demonstrated beyond any doubt, it made perfect sense.

It came at a time when many carp anglers were trying to get an edge by focusing intensely on bait, place or time – or all three. The route to a big fish was perceived to be through expensive prebaiting campaigns, access to exclusive syndicate waters, and/or dizzying numbers of rod-hours. Also under the 'place' heading was fishing at extreme long range, putting baits in places that had been hitherto unexplored. What led to the hair rig was a slight shift of focus, to another vital part of the fish-tempting equation: presentation.

Carp sometimes seemed to have an uncanny ability to tell hookbaits from loose offerings. There were stories of anglers going out in boats after a fishless session and finding their hookbaits untouched – but all the surrounding offerings gone. Initially it was thought that stiff monofilament poking out of the hookbait might be alerting the carp that this mouthful was different. Now we know that it's all to do with the way that carp feed – sucking the bait in, rather than moving to engulf it human style – and the behavior of the bait when they do that. This understanding has led to the further development of the hair rig to the point where the bait is given just the right amount of buoyancy to counteract the weight of the hook – a so-called critically balanced bait. With this refinement the hookbait now behaves in almost exactly the same way as a loose offering, when sucked or wafted by a hungry but wary carp. As an added bonus, and again making sense with hindsight, a hair rig gives a better chance of a hook-set than a hook nicked in the bait.

It also demonstrates that carp, at least, are less bothered by a hook that is supposedly visible than they are by a bait that behaves unnaturally. But many anglers, and otherwise knowledgeable fishermen I've met on my travels, persist in the assumption that a hook has to be buried in a bait. I'm often getting into discussions about this when I'm trying to hook a bait my way without hurting anybody's feelings. The only fish I've come across that seem to see hooks and be wary of them are goliath tigerfish, which sometimes take a precision bite out of a bait in the exact place where there are no hooks. But this is based on a very small sample size. Meanwhile in the Amazon, pink dolphins will clearly 'see' and avoid a hook even in muddy water, using their sonar, which is just as well because nobody should want to hook one of these 300-pound beasts. But if you cast in a dead fish with the hook just nicked into the lip, be prepared for a dolphin to grab the bait clear of the hook. The first time this happened to me I thought I'd lost the biggest catfish in the river. My boatman was laughing, and told me to look at the water. A few seconds later, the surface bulged and there was a loud puff of air. The sound seemed to carry a hint of mockery.

So much for the hair rig, other than to say that I had a nodding acquaintance with the man whose brainchild it reportedly was, the late Lenny Middleton, who I bumped into from time to time on a couple of waters. Most experiments, of course, don't have such revolutionary results. In fact most experiments don't lead anywhere at all. But a non-result is still a result. It yields information, which feeds into our evolving understanding of fish and fishing. So in my book it's always better to try something (time permitting) than it is to intend to . . . and then never get around to it. But perhaps I think about this more than most. Nothing concentrates the mind better than not having a 'next time.' But not everyone thinks like this. One fishing accomplice of mine used to occasionally indulge this experimental side to my nature, but when the experiment didn't work would declare, 'I *knew* it wouldn't work!' So I was always the person coming up with dumb suggestions. But I would still rather check something out, than just assume an idea has no value.

Many of my experiments these days concern bait presentation in moving water: If I moor at point A and cast to point B, the bait should settle somewhere, I reason, near point C. But I don't know whether it will unless I try. Often it doesn't work and I have to make adjustments, based on the new information I now have. Sometimes it now works, and sometimes it still doesn't, so I have to think again. Over the years, through repeatedly doing this, I've developed a greatly improved feel for the three-dimensional complexities of strong currents, and an ability to get baits to settle and hold position in places where appearances suggest that they wouldn't. Such places, of course, often hold big fish, and this approach has brought me a number of catches – notably goonch catfish, goliath tigerfish, and freshwater stingrays – that wouldn't have happened had I been less experimental in my approach.

Angling partnerships can also be great, sometimes, for the experimental process. You can bounce ideas around, spread your bets, and learn twice as fast. It's significant that the early specimen groups of the 1960s, which made such strides in big fish catching, operated on the basis of pooling knowledge. It's a bit like the way that science works, when working at its best. Then of course there's a wealth of written material, which is a good way to benefit from the experimentation of others. But the challenge is avoiding the temptation just to follow what other people are doing. Where angling gets interesting is in contributing to the overall body of knowledge.

One of my contributions is the following. Back when I was still carp fishing, I arrived at a new lake after dark. I walked around to the far side and set up in a spot where I could cast towards two islands: left-hand rod to one, right-hand rod to the other. Despite my excitement at fishing new water, the night was quiet, and for eight slow hours neither line moved. I don't know why the left-hand bait was ignored, but at daybreak the reason why the right-hand one was untouched became clear. Although some things seem obvious, sometimes our knowledge is increased by testing what we think we know. In this case the obvious wisdom was correct. Don't fish with your bait up a tree.

Twenty years later I was paddling a wooden canoe on a lake in the Amazon, casting a floating lure to the margins. In places fallen tree trunks sloped into the water. Elsewhere the lake was overhung by tangled vegetation, and it was to one of these areas that I now turned my attention, and cast. A little bit shorter and my aim would have been perfect. As it was, my lure was hung up on a thin branch, about a foot from the surface. With a grimace I remembered the leg-pulling jibe that a local fisherman had once delivered: 'Fishing for monkeys?' But this hang-up wasn't too bad, and I was using 80lb braid, so it was likely that a sharp pull would jerk it clear. But something stopped me. I would try something different.

Taking up the slack line I shook the rod-tip, making the lure audibly rattle. Seconds later a sinuous shape, gold in color and nearly a yard long, launched from the water and freed the lure for me. It was an arowana (*Osteoglossum bicirrhosum*), a surface-feeding predator well known for its varied diet – which sometimes includes beetles sitting on branches. Because of this habit it's also known as the water-monkey, and maybe that was the reason for my sudden impulse – and for the surprise catch that followed.

Be Opportunistic

The *tapah* were proving tricky. This is the name in Malaysia for a fish (*Wallagonia leerii*) that looks quite similar to the European wels catfish. That is to say it's a catfish with an elongated, somewhat serpentine body shape, as distinct from the more stocky-bodied species such as the North American blue, flathead, and channel catfish, and the South American piraiba. It's also called the helicopter catfish, for reasons I've never been able to discover, unless it's something to do with the very thin dorsal fin, which has just four soft rays behind the dorsal spine, giving it the appearance, if you use your imagination, of a propeller blade, or maybe a (short) helicopter rotor. Or it's one of those lost-in-translation things: an obscure local name somewhere, for this fish of many aliases, that sounds somewhat like 'helicopter.' A bit like what happened when my friend the late Barrie Rickards, the well-known pike-fishing guru and writer, came fishing with me in the Amazon, and feigned trouble remembering the name of one of the fish we caught. Thus the pirapitinga (*Piaractus brachypomus*, known elsewhere as the pacu, and notable for its human-like teeth) became the paramedic . . .

As usual, time was limited. I'd already searched the river with lures, casting from a drifting boat to all the likely looking holes along the overgrown and sometimes rocky banks, but without success. So it was time to defer to the local fishermen and concentrate on the handful of deep pools. Best bait, they assured me, was a livebait, ideally a smaller catfish.

The day before had started very hopefully. At a pool where the river turns a 90-degree corner there had been a swirl near the far bank. We'd quietly paddled into position upstream of this spot, and I'd drifted a bait down, suspended under a sliding float. After a long wait with nothing happening, suddenly the float wasn't there anymore. I waited then tightened, but back came just the bare hook. Kicking myself for not leaving it a fraction longer, I fished for the rest of the day without seeing any further activity. I started to wonder if I would look back on that as my only opportunity, missed because I did the wrong thing. Or maybe it had been a small fish, which couldn't take the bait in one go. That was my preferred belief, but I was still keen to come back to this spot again. So before leaving I did a quick survey of the pool with the portable sonar I had with me, and sketched the depths – mostly eleven to seventeen feet – to give me a better mental picture for a return visit.

On arrival the next morning we had a detailed plan, based on a better appreciation of the current and the underwater geography of the far bank. We would drift into a slightly different position, a little further upstream, and moor against a rock with the prow of the canoe protruding into the flow. From here I could much better control the drift of the float in the eddying current lines and thoroughly explore the zone where we'd seen the action. So we crossed the river with a minimum of disturbance, almost like a log floating down, and after some fiddly maneuvers on the other side we had the boat in the exact position I'd wanted. Holding my breath, I gently swung the bait out.

Scarcely had the float slid up the line and settled against the stop-knot, and swung into position on the current-edge, when there was a bulging swirl on the surface. But this was behind us, in a large slack upstream. It didn't take a lot of thinking about: I decided straight away to abandon our carefully set trap and reposition. That was a confidently hunting fish, active right now – a precise intersection of place and time. I needed to add a bait to the equation as soon as I possibly could.

We slipped back across the river, paddled quietly upstream, then slid across again and tied alongside some fallen branches. The strike had been just under the surface, so I set the stop-knot so the bait would work in the top half of the water column, and gently cast. We sat and waited, as the float slowly wandered in the lazy current of the eddy. Nothing. I recast closer to the semi-sunken tree on the outside of the bend, and after another uneventful half hour coaxed the float into a line of flow that took it close alongside a patch of clear, steep bank. Still nothing, and no further movements, but I was confident the predator was still down there. Slowly I brought the bait back towards me, until it was more centrally positioned in the slack, closer to where the fish had swirled. Trees closed in above the river here, but a fish looking up would still see a strip of sky, and from the bank-side edge of the slack it would be aware of the bait, from time to time, as a moving silhouette. There was no way it could not have registered. It was time for me to stop over-thinking, and just wait.

This is when, very often, I stop thinking like a fish – once the bait is in the water, and the trap is set. I bring my piscine alter ego back from the underwater realm, where it might bump into the fish I'm after, and let my mind go alertly blank. The origins of this date back to when I was in my late teens. At the time I was a newly joined member of the British Carp Study Group, and the group magazine was full of discussion about whether carp were telepathic. It wasn't just that thing of them waiting until you had a scalding hot mug of tea balanced on your knee before they went tearing off with the bait, but something altogether more profound. Unfortunately I can't look up the details now because I lent all my mags to somebody a few years ago and I haven't seen them since. But I've learned more recently that some subsistence hunters also believe that animals know when they are being hunted, purely from the hunter's thoughts. It's one of those things that sounds very unlikely, but although there is no known mechanism, it's also impossible to disprove. And because I'll take anything that might give me a small edge when it comes to catching fish, I will often emulate those primitive hunters.

So although I like to imagine myself under the water, as a means of working out where to place my bait, I often like to be in a different mental mode when the bait is out. It's a state of alertness and readiness, but I'm not thinking about the fish. It's a subtly different kind of focus: wide rather than narrow. I've no idea if it makes any difference at all to my results, but my hunch is that it does, because it makes me feel inexplicably more confident. As quantum physics has revealed, the presence or absence of an observer can change outcomes. Or regard it as just another kind of camouflage: dissolving into the background hum rather than loudly transmitting.

So instead of staring at my float I was taking in the whole

vista of the pool. It was simply a small red shape in an expanse of black water. And then there was no red shape. The braided line was sliding across the surface, making a miniature wake as it went, and pouring down a hole in the water's skin into that other world.

This time I had rehearsed mentally. I could see from the movement of the line that the fish was moving away from the bank, so no worry for now about snagging. I engaged the reel and waited for the line to tighten, and when it did I pulled back. Immediately it was clear, from the answering resistance, that this was a heavy fish, but from the boat I was in a good position to get control – a pull from directly above is hard for most fish to resist for long. Even so, it was a while before I saw the fish, dark against dark with a hint of a stripe. Not long after that, it was on the surface and ready for landing. One option was to make our way to the inside of the bend and beach it on the gently shelving sand, or I could use a gloved hand to grab its lower jaw, as one does for wels. But both of these entailed some delay and uncertainty (I hadn't yet seen how secure the hook hold was) and for this reason I had put a landing net ready in the boat, which my guide Roslan now lowered into the water. A few moments later he raised the net and we had it.

It weighed fifty-two pounds, and we had a program. An alignment of bait, place and time successfully achieved, which wouldn't have been achieved, possibly, if I'd stayed with my original plan. Which isn't to say that planning is not necessary. On the contrary it's vital – it's just that things will never be exactly as predicted. So although it's hard to know for sure, I put this catch down to being opportunistic. I saw a feeding fish and I reacted. The fish was telling me where to cast, and I listened.

— 19 —

Don't Think

I arrived at the lake in the afternoon, and was pleased to find that nobody else was there. I had plenty of time to set up before fishing the night. The question was, where?

There were only a few accessible spots, in gaps between the trees, and the favorite was where one of the banks bulged inward to form a point. From here it was possible to cover a variety of options: towards trailing tree branches on the left, off a big lily pad to the right, and into deep open water straight ahead. This well-trodden place was the obvious default, but it didn't really appeal, partly because of its popularity. I looked at the water and started to walk quietly around it.

Although I was alert to signs of fish – a fizz of bubbles, twitching weeds, a rocking of the surface – I saw none. But it was not wasted time. I had what I wanted.

Over the years I've become aware of something that I can best describe as an internal divining rod: something that, for no apparent reason, shifts my attention in a particular direction. When I look at the water I sometimes just have a feeling about a certain place. If asked to explain what factors might be responsible – wind direction? light? – I normally couldn't do so. On this occasion I found myself drawn to one of the lake's corners, around to the right of the point.

The water here was overhung by low branches. To reach it I had to take a small gap in some scrubby vegetation and descend several feet, to a narrow, sloping strip of spongy black soil, too small to put up my bed-chair and homemade brolly camp (in those days just a large umbrella with canvas sides stitched to it). The branches would make an overhead cast impossible, but distance wouldn't be necessary because there were only a few yards of open water before an expansive lily bed. It was no place to set up for the night, but my mind was made up.

Although this was before the days of rod pods, it was normal when static carp fishing to put out two rods, or sometimes three. Because of the confined space, I decided to stick to one. And no buzzer, because the bait would be mere feet from the rod-tip – just a small cylinder of crinkled aluminum foil hanging on the line.

When darkness fell, it was absolute. In the open there's surprisingly good visibility most nights, but under foliage it can drop to zero, or very close. Although many hours stretched ahead, I don't remember being uncomfortable or tired, because of my feeling that something was going to happen. I was confident that I was in the right place.

It was the rustle that first alerted me. A tiny sound, but one I'd become conditioned to react to. I turned my head and saw a ghostly patch of luminescence, where some of the stray photons that had made it through the trees were being reflected in my direction by my bite indicator. It was moving: slowly up, then abruptly down as a coil of line slipped off the open spool. My hand felt its way to the rod handle as I closed the bail arm and waited for the line to tighten. Out of nowhere came a weight.

In the darkness there were no dimensions, no layers. I couldn't see the rod against the sky, so I had to gauge where the fish was by feel – and by sound, when it sent up boils to the surface. I dropped the rod to one side then the other as it surged back and forth in the confined space, trying to keep it more confused than I was.

After an unmeasured time that was probably three or four minutes, I felt that it was tiring, and unlikely now to make it to the weed bed, as long as I kept a cool head. Then came a moment when I sensed a change: it was near the surface and its motive force was no longer convincing. With my left hand I reached for the landing net and slid it into the water, its forty-two-inch oak arms extending in a V-shape on the end of a six-foot handle. Now I raised the rod, directly above the net handle, to bring the fish towards the net's apex. Somewhere in my head I converted feeling and sound into a picture of shapes in the darkness, and judged the moment to be right. I lifted the net frame clear of the water, put down the rod, and got two hands on the job of securing the fish.

This was when things became confused, and didn't go to plan. The line seemed to be disappearing into the net, so the fish was in there, but the meshes were caught on a sunken tree root. When I pulled, nothing happened. If I pulled harder, I risked ripping the net and losing the fish.

While groping mentally for ways out of this impasse, I registered that more of the net was out of the water. Perhaps the root was bending, or about to break. I pulled a little harder, and the net came towards me. A bit harder, and it came some more. It was sliding up the mud towards the bank.

That's when I realized there was no root. What I felt was the fish, emerging from its weightless world, transitioning from zero to twenty-six and a half pounds.

Some anglers claim a mystical connection with fish, an inexplicable knowledge of where they are lurking. And sometimes it does feel like that, as it did that night at the lake. Despite my scientific background, I find myself listening out for an inner voice, a voice that sometimes insists on making itself heard, to pass on knowledge that comes from no discernible source. But I think there is a rational explanation, at least most of the time.

What I think is happening is this. We spend our waking hours constantly looking and observing, in a semi-automatic way. Who's that coming towards me? What time is it? Which way is that car going to turn? But there's also a lot of peripheral information that we take in below the level of consciousness. This information comes from all our senses, and may include such things as the smell of the air and changes in atmospheric pressure (felt in the middle ear, as changing tension in the eardrum). Most of the time this is just routine monitoring; it goes into a short-term mental cache, from where, normally, it is destined to evaporate.

In parallel with this collection of data, we are also analytical, reasoning animals. We see something that looks out of the ordinary and we ask why. We also maintain a mental model of the world, on which we run simulations: If I do x, what are the chances that this will lead to z, as opposed to y? All this is frighteningly complex, if we think about it too much, beyond the inner workings of any computer. It's software that has been shaped, just as surely as our bodies, by the unforgiving forces of natural selection. Testament to its effectiveness is the mere fact of our survival as a species, on a planet shared with other animals that are bigger, stronger, faster, better swimmers, better fliers etc. Many of these were intent on eating our ancestors, and the rest were highly motivated to avoid our ancestors eating them. If we think in terms solely of physical characteristics, humans survived against the odds, by undeserved fluke. But if we look beyond the physical, we survived – and dominated – by virtue of our onboard computers.

And the thing about all this data crunching and analysis is that much of it goes on below the level of consciousness. It's a back room that we never see inside. But sometimes a piece of paper is passed out of the door, or an answerphone message is left. Pick your own metaphor.

Sometimes the unconscious gives us answers in a dream, or a daydream. A famous example is the eureka moment experienced by the nineteenth-century German chemist August Kekulé, when he intuited the structure of benzene. The formula of this chemical compound had long been known to be C_6H_6 (meaning each molecule contains six carbon atoms and six hydrogen atoms) but the shape of the molecule was a puzzle. In school chemistry labs, such as the one where I briefly taught, complex molecules are often represented by 3D models of colored balls (atoms) held together by a network of struts (chemical bonds). Alternatively they can be shown as 2D diagrams. In a diagram a carbon atom is represented by the letter C, surrounded by four radiating lines, symbolizing four potential chemical bonds; and a hydrogen atom is the letter H, possessing just a single line. The challenge is to put six of one and half a dozen of the other together in such a way that all those sticking-out lines connect to another line, with none left over. To attempt this you don't even need to know any chemistry – it's the kind of logic puzzle you might find in the back of a newspaper. But until Kekulé cracked it, the solution had eluded the experts. The answer, once you've seen it, is blindingly obvious. The six carbon atoms form a hexagonal ring, with alternating single and double bonds between them. That uses up three of each carbon atom's four bonds, which leaves one bond remaining to link with one of the hydrogen atoms. For Kekulé, the ring structure came to him as a vision: of a snake eating its own tail.

But the workings of the mental machinery that delivers the dream, or the insight, remain unknown. We tend to visualize the space inside our heads as being made up of compartments: like rooms full of filing cabinets and display screens, linked by corridors and electrical circuitry – which doesn't quite fit with our other picture of it, as a couple of pounds of congealed porridge. Within this soft mass, neurologists have a partial idea of what happens where, but the relationship between structure and function is much more obscure than in a leg or a heart. So there is no clearly delineated box within a box where 'the unconscious' resides, although it can help our understanding to think of it that way, in the same way that it helps us to understand chemical compounds by seeing them as assemblages of ping pong balls and struts. But even though we don't know exactly where or how it happens, a lot of problems are chewed over in our heads without our being aware of it. The solutions float into our consciousness, as if from nowhere, sometimes as a coded message – a snake swallowing its tail – and sometimes as something more urgent.

At times the message is a matter of life and death. Stuck in my mind is a dramatic story I heard (I think on the radio) many years ago, and although I've forgotten the specifics of who, when and where, the *what* of this story is a dramatic illustration of how our minds can work. A racing driver was talking about a premonition that had possibly saved his life. He'd been speeding towards a bend when suddenly he felt – somehow knew for certain – that something was wrong. Against the all-powerful imperative to go as fast as possible, he eased up on the throttle, and coming out of the bend saw the chaos of an accident up ahead, which had been invisible to him before – and which he would have ploughed into had he still been traveling at racing speed.

Only later, using the racer's ability to decompress time, both in the micro-moment and retrospectively, did he work out the mechanics of that premonition. He'd passed that place several times before, but on this lap the pattern falling on his retina was abnormal. A band of color in the distance was dark instead of light. Not faces but backs of heads. Not looking his way, but at something up the track. So not pre-monition at all, but observation and reasoning, happening almost at the speed of reflex – and not involving the conscious mind at all until the very last nanosecond, when the motor neurons to the right foot fired their urgent command. Or maybe even this message took a shortcut . . .

All of which has no relevance to angling. Except it does. While few would challenge that anglers may be dreamers, any similarity with motor racing is less obvious, even though angling is sometimes described as a sport. One thing that is regularly trotted out, however, is that angling awakens the hunting instinct, but rarely does anyone consider what that means. Hunting is about acquiring protein and precious calories in the conveniently packaged form of the bodies of other animals. But those animals are understandably reluctant to hand those nutrients over, so hunting can be dangerous for the hunter. Venturing into the wild also makes the hunter vulnerable to other predators. One bad slip and you're done for. So it's a serious pursuit, and the angler who has a sense of this, I believe, who takes time to blend into the landscape and who goes into hunting mode, is more open to any signals that might arrive, from those deep and mysterious parts of our brains that are otherwise under-used in our modern lives.

Or the explanation of my catch was more mundane than this. The place I chose was not fished by anyone else, certainly not at night, because it was uncomfortable to sit there for any length of time. This, on a hard-pressured fishery, would make it a comfortable place for fish, where they would feel safe. But this reasoning came after my decision, a case of slow thought catching up with fast, unconscious thought.

Two nights later I walked around the lake again. This time the inner divining rod drew me to a place on the opposite bank, where a nearly dried-up stream bed created a damp gravelly strip at the water's edge. I could have reached the water here from the popular spot on the point, by belting out a long cast, but I enjoy the intimacy of close range so I decided to fish short instead, right in the shallows. As before, there was no space to set up as such, so I sat on the bank next to a single rod, oblivious to the discomfort because discomfort reminds us, sometimes, that this is real hunting. It's a special kind of empty time, in which every moment is full of possibility.

And again, during the night, the silver paper moved. Once more, after a tense struggle close in, the net slid into the water. Once more the meshes parted to reveal a large carp.

I recognized it by the scale pattern, just a token scattering on its dark, leathery skin. It was the same fish.

— 20 —

D. E. T. A. I. L. S.

I n the Kumaon foothills of the Indian Himalayas there is an ancient, long-lost tradition of buffalo wrestling. Actually there isn't, but it's possible that some future anthropologist will discover an echo of this strange custom in the region's oral history.

I'd been hearing stories about people disappearing in the nearby Kali River, and when I trekked into the valley a farmer told me he'd seen his prize buffalo dragged into the water while it was drinking. He never saw it again. The Kali is a powerful river, with whirlpools that appear from nowhere, and in places just one step can take you from three feet to thirty feet of water. The skeptical part of me said these disappearances were probably drownings. But I couldn't completely rule out the possibility that something pulled them in. Normally buffaloes wallow in water, but I never saw that on the Kali. And I never saw people bathing. They also had a plausible

culprit: a giant, hideous catfish known as the goonch. I'd
seen a photograph of a goonch seven and a half feet long,
which would have weighed some 300 pounds. Such a beast,
if it grabbed a pale foot waving in muddy water, thinking
it was a snack-sized fish, would have no trouble pulling the
foot's owner under. In fact a swimmer could easily be pulled
down by fish much smaller. A person in the water has very
little buoyancy; even a fifty-pound fish could overcome that.
Think back to school days and how easy it is to be ducked
in a swimming pool. But a full-grown buffalo is a piece of
living agricultural machinery, what they use in these parts as
a tractor, for ploughing the terraced fields. Standing in the
shallows, it would take a very big fish indeed to shift it.

If credibility has not by now been stretched beyond breaking point, this leads to an obvious question: How big could
a goonch grow? And the answer is, nobody knows. Fish are
very different from land animals in terms of maximum size.
Because their bodies are supported by water, they can keep
on growing, if their genes allow it and if they have a good
food supply. Once upon a time a twenty-pound carp was the
fish of a lifetime, then Richard Walker caught his forty-four-
pounder from Redmire Pool. Now, thanks in large part to
anglers feeding the water, we've seen a further doubling, and
more, of what is considered possible. In France and Hun-
gary, carp have now been caught over a hundred pounds. It's
what's known as indeterminate growth, and it's happening in
front of our eyes.

But the Kali is no longer a rich fishery. The populations
of smaller fish that goonch could feed on have declined over
the last century. This would seem to rule out any giant-sized
predator. But, say the locals, there is another food source that
could keep the mythical giant well fed. This comes in the

form of half-burnt human corpses from riverside cremations. The Kali is a tributary of the sacred Ganges, and it is Hindu custom to consign their dead to the river. And just in case I was wondering, which I was, they said there are no crocodiles here. The altitude is too high and the water's too cold.

The question I was asking myself at this point was the one I ask everywhere. What is the very biggest fish that I might hook? This wasn't just idle curiosity, but central to the decision of what tackle to use. Getting an answer is not an exact science. There is a lot of uncertainty and wild speculation about how big fish can grow. For a long time supposedly reliable sources said arapaima grow to fifteen feet long, which would equate to a weight of around 2,000 pounds. A more realistic estimate would be eleven feet and 500 pounds. When it comes to hard facts, rather than speculation, the biggest freshwater fish that has been fully authenticated was a nine-foot, 646-pound, algae-eating Mekong giant catfish, netted in Thailand in 2005. For goonch, which live in colder water and would therefore grow more slowly, I hazarded a top-weight guess of maybe 400 pounds. But size isn't everything. Some big fish can be brought in on quite light tackle, if the environment is user-friendly. The goonch is not one of those fish. They are negatively buoyant and have huge wing-like pectoral fins, which they use to stick themselves to the bottom. They are somewhat like a stingray on the line and getting them in is mostly a matter of brute force. So heavy gear, but how heavy?

Having first looked at kite cord and paracord, I ended up getting hold of some climbing cord in 4mm diameter, with a breaking strain in excess of 500 pounds. Because it wouldn't be possible to get any useful amount of this on a reel, it would have to be used as a handline. Purist anglers might want to look away now, but I actually like handlining. It's the most direct contact you can have with a fish, so in some ways it's the purest form of angling. (It's illegal in British waters, though, because it's a very short step from this to an unattended fixed line, or night-line.) And having once brought in a 200-pound arapaima using just hands and thick mono, without the cushioning effect of a rod or a reel's drag, I had some idea of what I might be up against. But that was in a shallow pool in the Amazon, not a raging mountain river. So we decided to rig a handline, complete with heavy-duty swivel and 350lb multi-strand wire, and give it, and me, a test.

Cue buffalo wrestling. More correctly it was a buffalo tug-o'-war. We would attach the wire leader to the buffalo's collar and see if I, with the help of seven young Kumaoni men, and the cord, could hold it. And we'd film it for posterity. In terms of simplified TV logic, if a fish could pull a buffalo, then my fishing gear needed to be in the buffalo-pulling league. To psych up the human team we did an elaborate Kumaoni take on a Maori haka. This all happened while I was making what would become *Jungle Hooks India*, a project that got off to an inauspicious start when our filming application got horrendously held up and we arrived in India several weeks too late. The snow melt on the Kali had already started, turning the water cold and grey, and since catching an eight-pound mahseer on day one I'd caught nothing further. With no fish showing on my line, we were desperate for any vaguely fish-related stories, and this was how we came upon this far-fetched tale of an alleged freshwater man-eater, and decided to investigate it further.

People, I suddenly realized, were yelling. Somebody had undone the tether holding the 1,000-pound animal to its post, and the coils of line on the ground were moving. I had to get to the other side of the line, but without getting my feet inside any of the coils. So I jumped across then grabbed the line at the precise moment it snapped tight. The next thing I knew, I was jerked through the air in a trajectory that dumped me down on my shoulder on the stony soil. As the pain shot through me, the others seized the line and for a moment everything seemed to hold. Then there was a loud crack, followed by the buzz of a heavy-duty swivel and half the wire trace blurring towards us like shrapnel.

Director and cameraman Gavin Searle, whose idea this had been, bounded up to me with a huge grin and the verdict: 'Short but intense!' Our second cameraman, meanwhile, was still waiting for his camera to switch on. We also had a belated briefing. The buffalo, we were told, was jointly owned by four families. His favorite family lived in a stone-built house that was just visible on a distant ridge. Everybody had predicted, but failed to tell us, that as soon as he was released he would immediately make a run for that house. They finally managed to coax him back that evening.

Although it's not something I'd recommend, the buffalo test is why I now use double-barrel crimps on multi-strand wire with complete confidence. They have become items that I rarely travel without: tiny, almost weightless things that have been key components for many big fish captures, starting with the goonch. But these crimps didn't arrive in isolation. My goonch campaign coincided with a big injection of fishing tackle know-how, which came at just the right time. Through my friend Tim Marks I met David Bird, now sadly no longer with us, the former match angler and angling advocate, who had latterly turned his attention, inventiveness and enthusiasm to big-game angling. David took my search for outlandish freshwater tackle utterly seriously, and delighted in being part of the plot to televise a monstrous goonch. He introduced me to wind-on leaders (which enabled me to fish a decent length of tough 300lb mono using a rod and reel), and provided me with all manner of large hooks and other bits and bobs that just weren't available in the UK back then, and still aren't. I ended up in the odd position of being a big-game gear aficionado who had never used any of this stuff in the sea. Since then, though, I've had a few opportunities to fish for exotic saltwater species. I've caught sailfish off Western Australia and striped marlin from Mexico's Sea of Cortez, and a big male tiger shark off Ascension Island, which tore the leader from the wire-man's hands an incredible nine times before we finally restrained it alongside the boat. But until I went to the Indonesian island of Sulawesi I'd never fished for those two iconic species, both capable of growing to over 1,000 pounds: black and blue marlin.

Having long ago read Ernest Hemingway's fictional account of this, in *The Old Man and the Sea*, I thought it would be interesting to try for one using a handline. Somehow we found a Chinese man who knew how to do that, and I duly found myself on the long journey out to the fishing grounds in his small boat. Once there we put out two large trolling lures: shiny metal heads trailing colorful plastic skirts, which popped and gurgled at the surface. The line, which looked to be about 200lb, was held on large wooden spools, and several yards of slack were carefully flaked out on the deck, well clear of our feet.

For a long time we criss-crossed the deep blue, scanning our wake for the tell-tale sign of a bill slashing the surface, but all was quiet. Then without any warning one of the lines was torn from the clip on the outrigger. My gloved hands tightened on the line as the boat accelerated, and I felt something like an aquatic buffalo before there was a sickening slackness. The line had broken.

A couple of hours later there was another hit. This time some loud yelling and hand gestures got me to let the line go, as the fish repeatedly flung itself into the air; and when I finally tightened down there was a solid weight on the end. After an hour of strategic boat maneuvers, during which I laboriously retrieved line, arm over arm, only to lose it again, I finally had the fish underneath the boat, with the line going vertically down. Slowly the fish came up . . . and suddenly it wasn't there anymore. The hook had fallen out.

And that was it. That amazing opportunity, to catch a marlin on a handline, won't ever come again. We did get some dramatic footage, though, of leaping fish and onboard chaos, so film-wise it wasn't too disastrous; but I was gutted – literally a feeling in my gut, which only got worse as I became wise after the event. Basically, on the first fish, the knot had failed, the one attaching the main line to the leader-swivel. I remembered looking at the knot before we started and seeing that it appeared to be just a load of half hitches. But thick nylon can be more forgiving than thinner diameters, and, besides, this was tried and trusted gear, so I let it go. When the broken line came in, however, the curly end left no doubt about where it had broken. Not only that: with a good knot, I'd have gone over the side before 200lb line failed.

For the second fish it's likely that the thick-wire hook never properly went in, because we never properly set it – out of fear of another break-off.

Looking back I realize that, now as then, part of me is trying to pass the buck, and find excuses. With no translator there was a language barrier, so the drill wasn't as clear as it should have been. Sometimes, too, there's no alternative to using somebody else's equipment, and on occasion this leaves something to be desired. Also, we were pushed for time, so I deferred to the local expert, because I'd never fished for big marlin before. But fishing a place regularly is very different from fishing there for one day. In the first case a win-some-lose-some approach can be acceptable; in the other case it isn't. But to work things through diplomatically, and develop a collaboration based on mutual respect, can take more time than is available. In the end, the specifics of this story are academic, and I need to own the mistake.

And that mistake is the biggest one there is. It's the mistake that makes a complete mockery of the fact that you did everything else right. Against the odds, you got 99 percent of the process right – bait, place, time, presentation – but that rogue one percent was not some random act-of-God glitch; it was something entirely avoidable. That one percent, which can make the crucial difference between fish and no fish, is the failure to pay attention to detail.

Number one detail is knots. Fishing tackle, like anything else, is only as strong as its weakest point, and that point is invariably a knot. However expensive and high-tech your rod, reel and other gizmos, a knot is something that you (normally) make yourself. So all anglers should be adept at tying knots. This is more than just a matter of knowing how to tie a particular knot. Sometimes a knot doesn't form perfectly. The nylon above the knot might look slightly constricted, or the wraps haven't settled evenly. At this point, assuming you have actually taken the time to inspect it closely, you either decide that it will do, or you decide that it won't. My normal approach is to retie if I have any doubt at all. Lubricate, pull evenly, then check again. Sometimes I'll do this four or five times, irrespective of whether anyone's tapping their foot or pointedly looking at a watch. When my line goes in the water, it could be there for several hours, and I might only get one opportunity. So I need to have full confidence in every component of my tackle, and no niggling worries that anything might let me down. It's a classic case of more haste less speed. If a big fish decides to run for a snag, I need to believe in my tackle's ability to stop it. Big fish are unforgiving, and will find and exploit any weakness. So if you're fishing without total confidence in your gear, you're asking for trouble.

The second big detail is hook sharpness. Many anglers assume that a new hook straight out of the packet must be sharp. In many cases this is true, but not always. Always check, and if necessary sharpen with a file. Sharpening technique takes practice, but basically it's a gentle stroking towards the point at a very flat angle: first on one side, then the other, then on the outside of the point. The difference this makes can be dramatic. But for many anglers hook sharpness, beyond a basic minimum, is never considered. Most fish are landed and some come off, and this is considered to be a normal, acceptable ratio. But the difference between catching difficult fish and not catching them is often about making small improvements in key areas. The mentality should be one of making every opportunity count, and taking every possible step towards that end. I remember an experiment I did years ago with a twelve-foot carp rod, 12lb monofilament and a spring balance. With the balance hooked into a loop on the end of the line I got my accomplice, standing fifty yards away, to strike as hard as he could. The balance barely read three pounds. That's why a sharp hook is important. Often on the strike, because of line stretch and/or a belly in the line, all that happens is the tiniest penetration of the very point. But that's enough; it will embed further if tension is kept up. But a hook that's not sharp enough will slide and fail to penetrate.

The hook should also be checked if there's any chance the point has bumped something on the retrieve and become blunted. If so, a touch-up with the file may restore the point. But if too much metal has to be removed, leaving the point significantly shortened, it's time to discard that hook and attach a new one. When selecting a hook, particularly one made from heavy-gauge metal, it's worth repeating that you should check that the eye is fully closed. If it isn't, look in the packet for a better one. If there's any chance of the line slipping through this gap, do something about it. Sometimes it's possible to reduce the gap using pliers. Or, as I've done in the past, tie a knot with a second piece of line to block this gap. Or fill the gap with quick-setting epoxy adhesive. If you're likely to re-use a hook (or a swivel) don't cut the line next to the metal. If the eye is scratched, this could possibly damage the line at the knot.

I also keep a close eye on the condition of my line. Suppose after catching a fish the last few yards are abraded. Sometimes this is just superficial; other times I'm not happy with it, so I take it off and retie the end tackle. I'll also check back several yards to make sure there's no other damage I haven't seen. When fly-fishing I've been drilled to regularly check for wind knots, those overhand knots that miraculously tie themselves, which can weaken the leader or tippet strength by as much as 50 percent.

I realize, as I write this, that some of these things may sound a bit obsessive, and unnecessary, but these details can and do make a difference. Whenever I'm fishing I want my confidence in my gear to be 100 percent. If it's not, I want to pinpoint where my doubt lies, and do something about it. Losing a fish through failure to check a knot, or the hook, or the line should never happen. Once is one time too many, simple as that.

Get everything right though, and it's amazing what fishing tackle will withstand. For a lot of the fishing I do, the weakest link isn't going to be the rod, or a knot. It's going to be me. While attached to a 153-pound wels catfish in the Río Segre in Spain, for example, using 150lb braid on a locked spool, I slipped onto my backside and was in the process of being pulled into the river – until my feet gained purchase on a slab of rock just inches from the water. If I'd gone in I could in theory have let go of the rod, but other similar instances suggest that I am genetically incapable of doing so. Other times I'm attached to the rod by a harness, and letting go isn't even an option. If the line were to dig in and jam, nothing is going to break: I'm going to join the fish in the water. In risk-assessment terms it's one of those low-likelihood/high-seriousness events. And because such an outcome wouldn't be good news, I carry a knife or line-cutter just in case – another small but important detail.

Meanwhile, every time I go fishing, I will continue to check those other vital details. Whatever the other uncertainties, I always want to fish in full confidence that there will be no equipment failure caused by human error. With this unexciting but vital component of my approach in place, I believe I have a fighting chance against anything that swims. Just don't talk to me about buffaloes.

SEA

— 21 —

A Sense of Scale

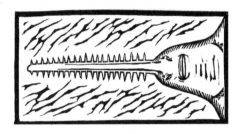

Catch-and-release fishing is such a bizarre idea to some people that it once got me arrested, and facing the very real possibility of rotting in a south-east Asian jail. I could sort of see their point. I had traveled halfway around the world to be on the Mekong River, in north-east Thailand, which I quickly found was full of gill nets and long-lines and consequently not many fish, and here I was telling locals that if I caught anything I'd put it back in the water, after taking a quick photograph.

I could see my story didn't compute. It had to be an elaborate cover for something else. After questioning me for a whole evening and most of the next day, the district police chief confiscated all my film and announced to his subordinates that they had just caught a spy.

The worst-case scenario didn't happen. I ended up being released and put on a bus to Bangkok with a police escort. On the way I gave him the slip and got on a different bus. This was stopped in the mountains by armed, uniformed men, who walked up and down the corridor looking at passengers before letting us continue. Once in the capital I went to the British embassy, to see if there was any way I could convince the authorities that I was just a tourist. I desperately wanted to salvage this trip, which I had financed by working for a year as a supply teacher in London, while lodging in a house that had many rent-reducing features, such as the absence of banisters in the three-story stairwell and plastic trash bags standing in for window glass in my attic room. After telling me to come back the next day, the embassy staff advised me to leave the country as soon as possible. It was a lesson in the unpredictability of the human environment, and one of my more bizarre blank trips.

It only made sense nearly ten years later, when I stumbled across some archived press stories. At the time of my trip the British government, it turns out, was secretly sending special forces to train guerrillas led by the infamous Khmer Rouge – who, after being ejected from Cambodia by the Vietnamese, were operating out of bases in north-east Thailand. If that's a hard one to take in, consider that the Vietnamese had recently humiliated the US in the Vietnam war (which ended in 1975), so in the eyes of some Western politicians that made the genocidal Khmer Rouge their friends – as long as nobody ever found out. So somebody wandering around north-east Thailand with a notebook and camera in 1984 would not have been welcome. In the end some real journalists unearthed the story in the late 1980s. Finally in 1991, after denying it for two years, the British government admitted to this less than glorious escapade – although by then few people in the outside world cared, or even noticed the story.

In the Amazon it was something different. Here people thought I must be an undercover gold prospector. But this didn't come with any kind of threat to me, just persistent requests to see what kind of firepower I was packing inside my suspiciously heavy rucksack.

But things are changing: the once inconceivable concept of catching fish and putting them back is gaining ground. For millennia, rivers and lakes all over the world provided enough fish not just for subsistence but also, very often, for some people to make a living as full-time fishermen, selling their catch to others. But the expansion of this industry, driven by human population growth and improved fishing methods, has now gone into sharp reverse – thanks to those very same factors. In just a handful of generations a wild freshwater fish for your dinner plate, if you want it, has gone from being a birthright to a luxury, and is fast going beyond that to something non-existent. This situation in our rivers shouldn't come as any surprise when you consider the more publicized state of the oceans – where at the current rate of exploitation there will be nothing worth fishing for commercially by 2050. If this can happen in the vastness of the oceans, then just reflect on the vulnerability of the fish in our lakes and rivers, which hold a mere 0.01 percent of the world's water.

In the places where commercial fishing on rivers is still a free-for-all, fishermen are scratching around for ever-diminishing returns. In western Zambia I've seen them reduced to using mosquito netting, to capture fish just a couple of inches long. Nothing gets a chance now to grow any bigger. Elsewhere long-overdue regulations and close seasons are attempting to save this way of life and the fish populations that it depends on. But enforcement is patchy, to say the least. There are a few success stories, such as the return of white sturgeon to the lower Columbia River in the north-west of the US in the second half of the twentieth century, but the populations of most river fish, it's safe to say, will never return to anything like 'natural' levels – whatever they were before people started harvesting them.

Most of this is going unreported. But my thirty-five years of travels have given me a unique window on things. Although scientists have scarcely studied what's happened to river fish populations, there is a rich oral history, everywhere in the world, telling the same story: of a precipitous decline in fish numbers and sizes in just the last hundred years or so. It's a decline that's confirmed by my own experience.

Although watching my *River Monsters* programs might give the impression that every far-flung river is full of man-sized beasts capable of biting your leg off or pulling you under, such fish are in fact very hard to find and catch. Many of the iconic underwater predators have all-but disappeared from most of their historic ranges. To find a large specimen you normally have to go to very specific, special places, normally where they have some degree of protection. Mere remoteness is not enough. And because many of the fish I go after are apex predators, the fish at the top of the underwater food pyramid, they are also indicators of the state of the river as a whole. If they are thriving, the chances are that so is everything else. But if they are missing, it is cause for wider concern. With this in mind, their absence from the places where they used to be found seems to point to a corresponding crisis among the supporting fish species. All this corroborates the sorry story that the old timers almost everywhere are telling.

This is the global context that recreational fishing – angling – now finds itself in. But many people have no idea how depleted and vulnerable freshwater fish are. There are still romantic, anachronistic notions about taking your catch home to eat. An extreme manifestation of this is found in Germany and Switzerland, where releasing your catch, if it is in season and over a certain minimum size, is illegal. Doing so can land you with a heavy fine or even in prison. So it's not just in places that harbor secret terrorist training camps where a catch-and-release angler can get in trouble with the police. This regulation purports to be about animal welfare: catching fish should be utilitarian, for food, and not about human enjoyment. But this justification unravels on closer inspection.

What's interesting is that culinary enjoyment is apparently OK. Or I might have got this wrong. Maybe you mustn't enjoy the taste, or at least tell the police that you don't, if they come asking. Although why anybody in twenty-first-century Europe would want to go to the time and expense of catching and eating fish that they find unpalatable is beyond me, when they can go hunter-gathering in a supermarket. From the point of view of the fish on the line, though, this is academic. Thanks to lobbyists who claim to care about animal welfare, the law decrees that it is kinder to kill a fish than it is to put it back in the water.

I find myself imagining what would happen in my home waters, here in the UK, if anglers had to kill and eat all the fish they caught, even if there was a minimum size. In the world of the people who frame the German and Swiss laws, the fish would keep on coming, from the miraculous under-water cornucopia. Meanwhile in the real world, the world of lots of people and not much water, I'd give it a year – if that – until UK waters were as good as devoid of fish. (Then people would give up angling, and at least there'd be no one to tell us that the rivers were dead, which would be a result of sorts.) That this hasn't played out so far in Germany is maybe, I'm told, because German anglers can be somewhat excitable and inattentive when they land a fish. And the fish, instead of accepting their legal status as meals-to-be, and dutifully lying still, sometimes wriggle out of their captors' hands and back into the water. Perhaps the fish welfare people should be on call to kill the fish themselves.

As a general trend, though, for all its strangeness as a concept, catch-and-release angling is on the increase in fresh water, in many parts of the world, while subsistence fishing and commercial fishing inevitably decline. And the reason is simple. Without people voluntarily returning their catches, fish populations in most places would be doomed.

For an angler, caring about fish numbers also has to translate into caring for individual fish. Some people argue that, to that end, we shouldn't catch fish at all, even if we justify it by planning to eat them. This is because a hook in the mouth would cause pain to a human, and so it's clear, so the argument goes, that it must be the same for a fish. But many fish put all sorts of spiky things in their mouths, things that I would defy any human to try to eat, such as live crabs and crayfish. Ask indigenous Australians what is the best bait for freshwater sawfish (*Pristis pristis*, elsewhere known as the largetooth sawfish), and they will tell you that it's a catfish. The catfish in question has three sharp spikes sticking out of its body: one on its dorsal fin and one on each pectoral fin. Each spike carries multiple barbs, plus a coating of toxic slime – it's like the most vicious treble hook imaginable. Yet sawfish voluntarily inhale the whole thing, to get at the catfish's juicy flesh. It really makes you think – or it should do.

Still with sawfish, when I was on the Fitzroy River in

Western Australia in 2010, filming with scientists from Murdoch University in Perth, we witnessed something else that challenges the assumption that fish sensations are the same as human sensations. With some fish it's easy to recognize individual specimens. Mirror carp are easily identified by their scale patterns, which are as distinct as any fingerprint. But with most species it's not easy to tell different individuals apart, if they are the same size. Sometimes there might be distinguishing marks, if you look carefully: the pattern of spots on a pike, a bifurcated tentacle on a catfish, a blemish somewhere on the body. If you have a good memory, or a good photograph, it's possible to recognize a capture as a known fish. But most people don't look at fish that closely, and wouldn't recognize a fish that they'd caught before. And they wouldn't be concerned about this, because to them it's academic – it has no practical relevance.

But it's not academic to academics. If scientists can recognize a fish as one that has been caught before, this can yield information about behavior and growth rate. (Has it stayed in the same area or migrated? Does it have a healthy food supply?) Meanwhile, the proportion of fish that are recaptures, versus fish that are showing up for the first time, gives an insight into population size. Lots of new fish indicates a large population, while lots of recaptures means a smaller population. But to get this info you have to positively ID the fish. Scientists do this by using tags.

Some modern tags are highly sophisticated, like the one we attached to a six-gill shark off Ascension Island. This recorded depth, temperature and light levels and transmitted this information to a satellite when it popped off and floated to the surface after thirty days. A tag like this costs a couple of thousand dollars, plus the satellite time, so scientists don't get their hands on very many. But tags for basic identification are much cheaper. The simplest is the spaghetti tag, which is anchored at one end under the fish's skin and trails a length of flexible plastic carrying a unique identification number and contact information. More pleasing cosmetically are microchip implants, similar to those used to identify pets, but you can only read the ID number if you have a scanner. For the sawfish, we were going low-tech, using plastic tags attached to the first dorsal fin.

The river had long been smothered in darkness when my line started running out. On my heavy gear the fight was short, but strange. I could feel a jarring side-to-side movement and something raking against my wire leader. Within a few minutes, a seven-foot sawfish was in the margins, at which point things got a bit more complicated. We had to extract the hook without getting sideswiped, get measurements and a fin clipping for DNA analysis, and get the tag in – all the while being alert for any saltwater croc lunging out of the river behind us. In other words, it was in everybody's interest to act quickly. Not for the first time, I wondered what the fish made of this procedure, this abduction and release by air-breathing aliens, and what would be going through its mind when it was once more at liberty.

What I wasn't expecting was what happened next. Within the next twenty-four hours, the same fish was caught again – twice – on handlines set by the indigenous Australian rangers who were working with us. Without the tag, we'd have assumed these captures were three different fish. This doesn't suggest a fish that is distressed, at least not distressed enough to pass up the chance of another free meal. I've witnessed a similar thing with carp in the UK (see Chapter 19), catching the same large fish within forty-eight hours.

I'm not inferring from this that catching a fish doesn't cause it any distress, but it does strongly suggest that this might be much less than many people assume. I've already recommended imagining you are a fish, as a way to locate and deceive them more successfully, but this only works if you remember the obvious: that fish are very different from us, in physiology and behavior. They are not people, and they don't have the same level of consciousness. But why stop the thought experiment there? When I try to inhabit the mind and body of a hooked fish, the thing that looms largest is not the hook, but the confusion, the unseen force. If the fish has not been hooked before, it has no understanding of what is happening – although it might have seen other fish behaving in an inexplicably agitated way, and have some realization that now the same thing is happening to them. And that thing, in their perception, is clearly a bad thing, so it will resist that force with all its strength.

This is another reason to use tackle that is appropriate. Get the fish in as quickly as possible, so it does not get too tired. The priority is to leave the fish as unaffected as possible by the process of being caught. To that end, also observe all the norms of good fish care. If it's a very large fish, it's best not to remove it from the water. Otherwise: a knotless landing net, then a smooth, wet surface (ideally an unhooking mat) and wet hands, to avoid removing protective slime. A moist cloth or part of the net over their eyes can also help to keep them calm, or at least ensure that they are shaded from bright light, if they have come from dark or cloudy water. Disgorger, forceps or pliers should be readily to hand, and the hook should come out easily if it is barbless or has a micro-barb or a barb that has been squashed down. Maybe pour some water over the fish to keep it wet, but the main thing is to be careful and quick. Finally, support the fish in the water until it can hold itself upright and swim off under its own steam. These are the basics, which most anglers should know.

Add filming to the mix and things get a bit more complicated. We want people to see the fish – really see it, in its entirety and up close – because in many cases viewers have never seen this animal before, and had no idea of its existence. Normally filming tends to be a stop-start process, often repeating the same thing several times from different angles – but that can't happen now. We have to get it right first time. Because we are dealing with a live animal out of its element and the clock is ticking, the process can have the feel of a Formula One pit stop, with the camera just picking up whatever shots it can. So compared with other parts of the program, the climax can seem a bit ragged; but this, to my mind, better conveys the emotion of the catch, and underlines the importance of returning the fish quickly.

In fact, so important is a speedy release that we sometimes employ trick filming to achieve this. It's something I don't mind owning up to, and explaining. Normally the final, edited version of me holding a fish, and talking about it, cuts between three kinds of shot. First, a wide shot of me plus the whole fish, to show its size. Second, close-ups of the fish, to show features such as eyes and scales. Third, close-ups of my face, looking down at the fish and up to camera, to deliver information. At times the tight shots of me are not all they seem. If you were to pull out, you would see that I'm not holding the fish at all, but something like a heavy plastic box. The fish has gone; it's back in the water, and we're doing this after the event. So it's slight fakery, but it gives the fish early freedom. I like to think that anglers will forgive this slight dishonesty.

But caring about fish inevitably brings us into deeper water, where suddenly we feel out of our depth and conflicted. If we profess to care about fish but don't care about the state of the water they live in, and the effects that our multitudinous waste products are having on that water, then that is an inconsistent position. I get the feeling though that many people, and not just anglers, do care about this; but this is not as evident as it could be because of widespread self-censorship. This is because anyone questioning the rationale of ever-increasing consumption tends to be portrayed as an extremist who wants to force everyone to live in caves. It's a crude but effective misrepresentation, which makes people mostly keep their heads down – and it also deflects attention from where the real fundamentalism lies. (The other common misdirection is to change the conversation to one about over-population, and to blame the planet's problems on people who, per capita, consume next to nothing.) But what alternative is there on offer to the central belief of the world's new fundamentalist religion, that ever increasing consumption is perfectly compatible with a finite planet?

The central problem is that governments, even those that are nominally democratic, are primarily answerable to the owners of capital. Because of this, they don't just protect capital; they promote its relentless concentration, by keeping everybody else in debt, and dutifully paying interest throughout their lives. And one way to keep creating this debt is to drive consumption and waste. So don't expect any change from business as usual anytime soon, at least not in the top-down direction. Meanwhile any call for some new and more imaginative thinking is met by a diversionary lecture about jobs, although these are conveniently forgotten about at other times. Whatever happens, of course, we have no choice but to be consumers. We all need a place to live, food to eat, the means to move around, and occasional entertainment. But within these areas, and elsewhere, we do have considerable choice, to operate in a way that is more truly democratic, a way that works from the bottom up.

All of which is easy for me to say, but how do I square this with flying tens of thousands of miles every year with five or six other people and their baggage? As it turns out, there are those in the film and television industry who recognize that it's time to try to operate in a different way. The production company I work with is signed up with a pioneering UK-based scheme (wearealbert.org) whereby all the company's productions calculate and report carbon usage. In doing so they aim to reduce the environmental impact of the whole production process – everything from using refillable water bottles and not using disposable plastic to keeping travel miles down by employing in-country crew members. And in my personal life I try to further redress the balance. My car is nearly twenty years old, but because it still works I am loath to throw it on the scrapheap. And although I eat meat, I do so very rarely, which goes a little way to reducing the amount of the earth's surface that's given over to growing crops to feed livestock. (Recent studies reveal that cutting down on meat and dairy products is the single biggest thing that most of us can do to reduce our impact on the planet and its wild animals.) It's another checklist running quietly in the background, a personal audit, which is not about being uncomfortable and miserable, but shaving back, here and there, on unnecessary consumption and wastefulness.

It comes down to thinking independently about how we act, which should be the big thing that angling teaches us to do. Instead of defining ourselves, and others, according to what we possess and how much we spend – our obsession with numbers again – we can try to tread a little more lightly on the world. We don't have to live in caves, and renounce the benefits of technology. But we can go against the direction in which we are being pushed, and dial back, even if it's just a little, on our consumption and our dependence on possessions. It's a scary idea, because it goes against how we've been conditioned to address our insecurities. But if we each do what we can, all the untold millions of us who despair at the world's present trajectory, the cumulative effect is not so small.

It's something that could help the fish, and us, be around for a little longer.

— 22 —

(Notes to Self)

We think we'll remember everything important but we don't. We need extra capacity for the things that will, over time, fade, degrade, corrupt, and plain drop out of our heads. Some of those things will be details of our time on the water that may help us to catch fish in the future. How did I rig that bait, exactly? What strength line did I use to attach the weight, so it would break free if it became snagged – but not snap off on the cast? How many seconds did I let the lure sink, before I started to retrieve? What was the weather like when that fish finally took?

To keep a hold on these details, we need an external device to back up our onboard memory, something we can plug in when required. Personally I'm a fan of fused cellulose-fiber mat technology, otherwise known as a notebook, of the non-electronic kind.

But writing a blow-by-blow account of each day's fishing

would take forever, so it's necessary to apply a filter if you don't want to succumb to information overload. I've been keeping fishing diaries since my mid-teens, which gradually morphed into fishing/travel notebooks. They started off brief and succinct, in tiny, neat handwriting, with occasional mini-essays when I caught something. Then they became a mix of methodical and rambling, complete with maps, diagrams, shopping lists, squashed bedbugs (entombed in black insulating tape), fish scales, bits of line, the bloodied thorn that stapled my heel inside my shoe on an Indian hillside, and the hook (comically small by my current standards) that brought in a ninety-two-pound mahseer. More recently, though, they have lapsed back into brevity, with gaping gaps, the result of crammed schedules and sleep deprivation. A lot of what's written is also illegible, which I used to think was just me, until I discovered that the four rules for political diaries – the 'Four Is' – as codified by Gyles Brandreth and Alan Clark, are: immediate, indiscreet, intimate and indecipherable. I too was writing personal thoughts that I didn't want anyone else to read, at least not until I was ready. What many of those thoughts were is anybody's guess, because I still can't decipher them. But secrecy was a wise precaution. One day my uncle saw (over my shoulder) one of my carp bait formulations, and commented on the inclusion of 'ingredient X.' My uncle didn't fish, but he might have met somebody in a pub who did. As it is, the identity of ingredient X remains a secret to this day. And no, I'm not going to reveal it now, because I don't think other carp anglers ever got onto it. It might have some mileage one day.

What all of this boils down to is: I'm still trying to get it right. But having run the whole gamut – from obsessively detailed through brief and semi-legible to nothing – I think I'm now in a good position to give some good advice, to others and to myself.

The first thing is to have some consideration for your future self, the self who might be poring over these pages in weeks or months or years to come, searching for some vital scrap of information. To find something in a landscape you need landmarks, and when the landscape is 192 pages of words in a notebook the best landmarks are dates. My most easy-to-navigate notebooks have the dates in capitals (*FRI 25TH APR*) and enclosed in a box, to make them stand out from the surrounding scrawl. Also 'boxed' are places (*MOVED TO HAIRA*), significant captures, and other notable events (*Elephants – everywhere! [no fishing]*). These are from an A5 hard-bound book, identified by a label on its battered cover as *INDIA 86*. As well as being signposts, these also provide the basic when/where/what information that forms the framework for recording any story. (Just add who, why and how and you have the 'Five Ws' checklist used by journalists and police investigators.)

Other than making this information stand out, it can be pretty free-form, in as much or as little detail as seems appropriate, but I'll normally start with a note about tackle. It's rather like writing up a scientific experiment ('equipment,' 'method' . . .), which makes sense because, actually, that's what it is. With every cast we're testing a hypothesis: If I cast *this* bait *there*, there's a better than random chance that a fish will take it. This is where I'll often draw a quick labeled diagram of the terminal tackle, to show leader material and length, hook size, weight – every component. There's another 1,000 words to be saved by sketching a rough plan of my fishing spot, showing current, approximate depths, features and snags, my position and the places where I cast.

Then there's bait. On the night of 7 September 1972, at an Essex sand pit, I set up next to some sunken *tree trunks, car doors etc.* and cast out a crust-balanced 'special' bait concocted from: *"Oxo", "Pal", 3-day-old cat food, sardine and tomato paste, cheese, flour, bread, toast, mouldy bread and dog biscuits.* Sometime after midnight this tempted a smoky-grey mirror carp of 12lb 2oz. Nowadays I'm more likely to rig deadbaits, sometimes in strange and unorthodox ways, determined by whatever bait I happened to get hold of and the oral anatomy of the fish I'm after.

Recording these things helps to make me question why I am employing this method. Because it worked in the past? Or – much more interesting – am I trying something new? If so, based on what thinking exactly?

Usually I'll make these notes after I've brought in my line, by the light of a campfire or a headlamp. But I still like to have my notebook with me on the bank, to jot key things as they happen: fish size, time of capture, weather changes. Maybe water temperature, barometric pressure and moon phase too. Water level can also be crucial: in parts of the Amazon the seasonal rise and fall can be as much as fifty feet – but a fall of just one foot can be the signal to hurry to a specific lake. Then there's visibility, which can dramatically affect the willingness of some fish to feed. So I look and note. For this reason I now favor the more portable A6 size, hard-bound and with pen holder attached.

Looking back is the time to fill the gaps. I jot a brief summary of what happened in an abbreviated style, not worrying too much about grammar, just getting it down. Often this is not sequential; it jumps back and forward, as things jump into my mind. Such as the submarine driving past, as I sat with my lines reaching down to the bottom of the fjord.

Now is also the time to come to some kind of conclusion. Did the original hypothesis prove correct? No fish doesn't necessarily mean no. It may be a case, simply, of persisting – of waiting for the right time. Or a new idea comes to mind. Either way, a few minutes going back over the day makes me interrogate my fishing more. In order to arrange words I must arrange thoughts. Like drawing, it also makes me observe more closely, and try to understand what I see. It's an antidote to fishing on autopilot. And this, even if I never refer to them again, makes my note-making worth doing.

But I do go back to them, not just to confirm odd facts when I'm planning to return to the water, but to savor those times again:

Felt v. small fish but suddenly went solid made powerful surge to left – line got caught around tree – went in after it (up to neck) freed line and subsequently landed fish after about 6-7(?) mins total. (Oxfordshire, 1976) . . .

NO RAIN – BUT RED WATER COMING . . . Don't forget PALUDRINE TABLETS – after breakfast . . . 16lbs – razor pool. Dynamite gang (6) apprehended. (India, 1986) . . .

Chef (on seeing heavy line on table – 40/45/50) "C'est la vrai guerre." (Congo, 1991) . . .

Dry season is Jun/Jul/Aug until Dec. Lots of fish (pacu) caught in channels at this time. On small live fish. Also on dead Java carp fished from houses at Yigai – at night after village has quietened down. (Papua New Guinea, 2010) . . .

Wanted to get one of the brown ones out and they were

around but another good sized one was positioned as shown. Let it take well, gently tighten, then up onto bank 51 inches (measured by hand) – about 15lbs ?? . . . Vic: *"They are scary things. They have huge power and come out of nowhere."* (New Zealand, 2010) . . .

SQUID BOAT. Maria Felix IV (escorted by MFV & Guardacostas) skipper talking to other captain who caught 89kg POTA 2yrs ago – sin vísceras (est 8kg) = 97kg total. ie well clear of 200lb. (Pacific Ocean off Peru, 2015) . . .

Zhōng huá xún – Chinese sturgeon. Bái xún – Chinese paddlefish . . . He thinks paddlefish are still there. They've picked up fish on sonar – can't be sturgeon because they "can't get over the dam." – Saw the last paddlefish to be seen. "very beautiful" . . . Tracked with acoustic tag for 2 days then lost (river v high/fast at time). (China 2017) . . .

I don't know what it is, but I find there's something about words that brings it back more powerfully than a photograph or video. The best pictures are in my head, and words bring the mental projector to life. As our symbiosis with electronic recording devices shades into parabiosis, we risk our memories becoming pale, generic things. It's inviting a kind of blindness. Words keep the imagination alive.

They also lead to unexpected places. The first time any of my words appeared in print was a letter I wrote, in my early twenties, to the British Carp Study Group magazine. The next step took a few years. After returning from India in 1982, I managed to sell two articles to a fishing magazine, for forty and twenty-five pounds. This was when I first had the idea that my interest in far-flung fish might parlay into some kind of career. That turned out to be a bit over-optimistic, as I'm still waiting for the second payment. But I carried on: twenty years of traveling and fishing and writing it down, in between spells of being a teacher, advertising copywriter, barman, newspaper reporter, café worker and the rest. What I was also doing, I now see, was placing baits. A newspaper article here, a photograph there. Words and pictures. Glimpses of stories. Over time, the circling started and drew closer. I twitched the line and waited some more. Lady luck smiled, and the rest, as they say, is history.

But although I now inhabit a different medium, I still carry my notebook everywhere. To the point where it has become something of a trademark, like Sherlock Holmes's magnifying glass. And it symbolizes the same thing: that every visit to the water is an investigation.

A notebook, for me, is also what transformed my fishing. And carrying it is a reminder of this: of the benefits, big and small, and sometimes unexpected, of trying to write it down.

— 23 —

I'm More Uncompetitive than You

The water in Oklahoma is surprisingly cold in the spring, if you've been immersed in it for a couple of hours. Even with a shorty wetsuit under my clothes, I was shivering and wanted to get out. But I kept shoving my arm into hollows under rocks, and inside the rims of sunken truck tires. I was getting more miserable and despondent by the minute. We needed a fish but nothing was biting.

It was my first attempt at catfish noodling: no rod, no line, no bait. Actually that's not quite true: I was using myself as bait, specifically my hand, although a foot can work just as well. But I was not baiting in the normal sense, of offering a tasty treat. I was baiting in the sense of annoying, goading, or provoking. In the dark confines of the catfish's nest the hand is an uninvited intruder, and the bite is an act of aggressive defense.

I'd been hearing from old hands what this kind of bite

feels like. If the fish takes you in deep and then spins, they said, its tooth pads will turn your forearm into hamburger meat. One man had his size-twelve army boot engulfed by a massive fish, which held him with his head under the water until his buddies rescued him. But a catfish bite can be preferable to the alternatives. There's always the chance that your chosen hole is home to a beaver, or a water moccasin, or a hundred-pound snapping turtle. So I was nervous. But I also wanted to get it over with, and get warm.

As the hours and days passed, however, it became clear that the catfish just weren't there. Nesting is a seasonal activity. When the water starts to warm, the male fish finds a suitable cave and proceeds to tidy it up, sweeping away silt with his tail until the floor is clean and firm. Then it's a case of waiting for a female to show up, spawning, and guarding the eggs. A trained human eye can spot many likely nesting places. Other spots are found by feeling around underwater. This can also yield other information: if the floor of the hole is silty, nobody's home. And if, as I was finding, nobody's home anywhere, no amount of trying harder is going to bring a result. Fishing at nearly the right time, in this case and many others, is fishing at the wrong time. And we were there, for various reasons, at the wrong time. We would have to rearrange my schedule and come back.

Oklahoma take two. Tiny puffs of cloud drifted through the sky, giving no shade from the sun. The river was shrunken – in its box, as they say in the Amazon – and the water was comfortably warm. My two companions, Nate and Dillon, were explaining tactics for our first spot. This was a length of concrete pipe, angling down into the water. The bottom end was partially embedded in the riverbed, which had been excavated and landscaped to create a bespoke catfish love-nest, with a raised threshold and a deep hollow behind. The opening was too narrow for a torso, and an arm wasn't going to have enough reach, so Dillon, being the most slender, was going to put his legs inside.

The species we were after, the one most commonly fished in this way, was the flathead catfish (*Pylodictis olivaris*). The most secure place to grab one is by the protruding lower jaw, which is like an oversize suitcase handle, but it must be gripped very firmly, so the teeth can't rasp. Because of the fish's underbite, plus the upward angle of the pipe, Dillon turned face-down before ducking underwater and reversing himself in, having first taken a deep breath. Almost immediately there was a dull thud and an eruption of water inside the pipe. A fish had reacted. Dillon's head appeared, gasping, just above the surface, and I went under to secure and retrieve the pinned fish. This all went well until the fish's body was clear of the pipe, at which point it took all three of us, with a combined weight of over 500 pounds, to subdue forty pounds of fish and get the stringer cord threaded.

Five minutes later we let it go. Nate reckoned it was too small to get us a top place in the competition. We were after something bigger.

Prior to this, I had entered a fishing competition just once. A friend of mine belonged to his work fishing club, and he invited me to a club match, at a gravel pit in the Cotswolds. By fishing very light, I managed to catch a number of tiny rudd, and at the weigh-in I was surprised to learn that my total weight, barely a pound if I remember correctly, gave me second place, just fractionally behind the winner. This was when I realized that more fish had gone into my keepnet than had come out. Some of my fish had been so small that they'd swum out through the holes. (This was before the days of fine-mesh knotless nets.) At the time I joked about it, missing out on my rightful first place. But, I wonder, does the fact that this memory is still there, while many others from that time have completely evaporated, say anything about me?

Our next catfish spot was very different. Walking barefoot along a sandy beach we arrived at the outside of a wide river bend. Here the bank was a steep earth cliff fringed by a flat ledge, where the crew set up. For several feet beyond the water's edge the river was shallow, less than knee deep; then there was a drop-off, to more than waist deep. Just beyond the drop something poked through the surface. It was part of the mangled and rusting skeleton of a wrecked car, possibly dumped by a farmer years ago to try to slow the erosion of the bank.

Easing ourselves down into the brisk flow, the three of us took up position tight to the drop-off. Nate had just given me a briefing, using a diagram drawn in the sand, explaining that the catfish hole was in the face of the drop-off. It was an arch-shaped opening, and we were right in front of it now. He had been pretty certain there would be a fish there, and this was confirmed when suddenly something rammed our legs. This time it was my turn to go and get it.

There's an important point of technique with noodling. When you reach into the hole your hand should be horizontal but your thumb should be pointing down, in contact with the riverbed. This way, the catfish can't bite beyond the palm of your hand. This makes it easy to grab by the jaw and avoids harming the fish – unlike the regrettable practice of some noodlers, who will grab the gill rakers, which is no good for catch and release. The next thing is to stop the fish spinning, which is its default reaction to being grabbed. I had to be ready to pin it to the floor of the cave, or the wall, and at the same time reach forward with my other hand and grab the root of its pectoral fin. Otherwise, in the worst case, it could twist and pin me.

'Every year people die noodling, from drowning,' Nate had told me. 'Sometimes their head's close to the surface, and they just can't quite get there.' It's the main reason you shouldn't do it alone.

With all this firmly fixed in my mind I ducked under. I couldn't even see my hand in front of my face so I had to find the entrance by feel. Making sure I trailed my thumb, I followed the slope down from the threshold. I was wearing gloves for protection, but my fingertips were bare – all the better for feeling fur, snake scales, or a turtle shell. But I felt nothing, just mud. My air was running out; it was time to come up.

The entrance, I now knew, opened out to a very big space, and I hadn't been in there far enough. I needed to get right inside. But how would I get out if my hands were full? We decided that Dillon would hold my ankles, wheelbarrow style, and pull me out when the time came. But how would he know when that was? We agreed I would shake my right leg, slowly for a slow extraction, quickly for quick. Then I had to reload the basics: mainly the whole thing about overriding the normal common-sense reflex, of trying to whip my hand away if it got bitten. I also had to avoid getting caught on tree roots or other snags.

Because it was likely I'd be in the hole for some time, I started the breathing routine that I use for breath-hold diving. This is not to be confused with hyperventilating, which is potentially dangerous because it gets rid of carbon dioxide from the bloodstream, and with it the body's need-to-breathe safety mechanism. Instead, this is all about breathing slowly and deeply to get the blood as fully oxygenated as possible, and to bring the heart rate down by calming the mind. I'd done some timed breath holds earlier in the day, lying on the ground and slowly increasing up to three minutes. This would translate to a confident minute or maybe ninety seconds underwater. Now, breathing from my diaphragm, I did one final exhale, pushing out everything I could, followed by a final, super-full inhale. Then under.

With limited time, I couldn't afford to be too cautious. The space kept going back and the darkness was absolute. But my fingers would be visible, perhaps, to a dark-adapted eye – belonging to something the size of a dog, something which could be in front of me right now. Or it would lock onto my hand because of its movement, the disturbance it caused in the water. I tried to visualize it as I told myself to be ready. Any moment now . . . and *you must grab it back* . . .

I was in past my waist, feeling the entrance brush my thighs, when it happened. It was a sound, a muffled explosion, as much as it was a clamping on my hand. I gripped in response and pushed down, as an inner voice took control: pin it to floor – other hand grip fin – shake leg slowly. As it came out I kept it wedged against the wall of the cave. Then I was in a position to get my head out and above the surface, in preparation for bringing the fish into the open. Here my plan was to step over its body and get it in a scissor grip, while the others supported me and put the stringer in. The fish, as expected, wasn't co-operative. It was nothing like a fish that has been tired out on a line; at one point it even managed to put me in an arm lock, by twisting my wrist, before we had it secured.

All this above-surface chaos was recorded from the water's edge by our veteran cameraman, Duncan Fairs, but the real action had been out of sight, underneath the ground where he stood. I asked if they'd managed to pick up the sound of the fish biting down. 'Hear it?' said Duncan. 'I felt it through my legs!'

At the weigh-in the fish went fifty-three pounds, and we ended the day with a total of 155 pounds for our top three fish. This gave us top place in the competition, which was organized by a local church.

Since then I've caught a lot of other fish, but to this day that brown, somewhat slug-like 'mudcat,' pulled from the darkness of an underwater cave, is one of the catches that most sticks in my mind. But that's nothing to do with winning the competition, and making good on my previous second place. There are other reasons. Recalling it now makes me think, and not for the first time, about why I fish.

When I first started fishing, I was spectacularly unsuccessful. One early spot was a shallow, clear cut off the Suffolk Stour, which ran through the village where I lived. Here I could see the fish darting between weed beds, but they never came near the lumps of bread that I flung at them. So I cast into the big river bend near our house, but my float stayed motionless. Nobody in my family fished, so nobody could tell me what I was doing wrong. I was just going through the motions, putting a line in the river because it was something that most village boys did at some point, 'because it was there.' It was a minor rite of passage, something which most duly passed through and then left behind. I nearly left it behind too, for the more exciting pastimes of tree-climbing, riding my bike, and clambering around on the forbidden scaffolding of building sites. In comparison, fishing seemed like an elaborate waste of time. But that changed when I finally caught a fish.

My school friend Simon knew how to catch fish because his grandfather was an angler. Near his house there was a semi-collapsed wooden bridge, overlooking a channel of dark, reed-fringed water. Here Simon lent me some gear that was more fit for purpose than my cheap plastic combo, gave me some basic instructions, and – hey presto! – there was a finger-sized roach flashing silver in front of me. I don't know what exactly happened in that moment, in the recesses of my seven- or eight-year-old mind, and I had even less idea then, but it was like switching on an internal magnetic field, which was to exert a pull on the direction of events from then on.

At first it was just the novelty of catching any fish at all: gudgeon, perch, dace, more roach. And for a long time that was enough. I was aware that some people caught bigger fish, from other places, but that was a different reality from the one I inhabited. I tried to imagine a four-pound tench, what the pull of such a monster would feel like, before it inevitably broke my line. Then, from somewhere, I started to hear about 'specimen hunting,' the targeting and catching of big fish by design rather than by accident. At first it sounded unlikely: surely these people were just jackpot winners claiming, after the event, to have a system. Was it possible that there could be a system? I started some more in-depth reading of angling newspapers and magazines.

Thus began my pursuit of bigger fish. The system started, I learned, with stealth, patience, research, and belief. It was the beginning, and it started to work. From time to time I caught a fish that took two hands to hold. Among them was my first pike. At four pounds it was not a big one, but it was my first up-close contact with a predator. As such, it operated another internal switch: it activated that latent fascination with predators that we all have. It was a subtle but irreversible reconfiguration that would take me half a lifetime to understand.

Somewhere in that time I became aware of a fundamental division that was said to exist in British coarse fishing. At the other end of the spectrum from the specimen hunters were match anglers, who fished for numbers of fish, in competitions where the placings were determined by aggregate weight. And in this division I became aware of a certain snobbery: the fact that many big-fish anglers looked down on competition anglers, not because of the small size of the fish they caught, nor because of any shortcomings in their ability to catch fish, but because match anglers are, by definition, competitive.

I confess to getting caught up in that snobbery, which also extended to 'pleasure anglers,' the big group in the middle that included my younger self, in which I still had one foot if truth be told. The official line, with us specimen hunters, was that we weren't competitive. Or if we were, we were in competition with the fish, whatever that meant. But something about this didn't add up. A three-pound roach is a massive roach, but a three-pound pike is a tiddler. But how we know whether a particular fish is big or not is only with reference to what other people are catching. So our credo was built on an inherent contradiction. Just because we deny our competitive nature doesn't mean that it doesn't exist.

In fact the competitiveness of specimen hunters doesn't bear much comparison with that of match anglers. In a fishing match, where competitors fish at the same time in the same water, drawing lots for randomized pegs, it's the closest thing possible to a controlled experiment, where the only significant variable is the anglers' differing levels of skill. Big-fish anglers don't want to fish like that, which is fair enough, but our playing field is a complex landscape where the angler's ability is but one of many variables. Chief among these are time and place. Some people spend much more time fishing than others, and some places are not open to all. Many anglers, being thoughtful people, acknowledge this and attempt to address it. Some carp anglers go for big fish that have never been caught before; others target big fish from public waters. This is consistent with an old saying about a fisherman's progress: that our obsession moves on from any fish to the biggest fish – and thence to the most difficult fish.

This is where it gets interesting, because it moves us into an area where objective measurements don't exist. Even at a point in history where almost every aspect of our lives is reduced to numbers and governed by algorithms, it's a place beyond all this, where other values still hold. There are no universal gauges of difficulty, no quantitative comparisons. It is up to us, individually and subjectively, to decide what is meaningful and what isn't.

For me, I remain in thrall of big fish – I can't shake that – but what sets a capture apart is its story. Many of the best stories are about testing limits, overcoming fear perhaps, or exhaustion. Sometimes the story is a lesson, or a parable. And sometimes you can't put your finger on why a particular story has such power. It's just something you feel, personal to you, beyond numbers and words.

A fifty-three-pound flathead catfish is a respectable fish, but not exceptional. It's less than half the size of the rod-caught record. Thinking about it now, I could probably have caught it on a line, by threading a heavy rod into that underwater hole. That would have made quite a story.

But it would have been a lesser story.

— 24 —

Going Under Again

I dislike the term 'extreme angling,' which is sometimes applied to what I do. But I can't think of a better two-word summary, so I'm stuck with it. The idea of doing things that are off the normal spectrum, however, greatly appeals to me – although when it comes to putting that idea into practice, it sometimes gets complicated. Some things are only enjoyed retrospectively.

Possibly the most extreme fishing I've done was sending a bait down more than 2,000 feet into an oceanic trench. A line wasn't necessary because I was going down there with it. We were trying to film six-gill sharks (*Hexanchus griseus*), a deep-water species that is rarely observed. Diving was out of the question for the depths that would be necessary, but then somebody came up with the idea of a submersible. The problem was finding a vessel available in the right place. And the other thing, when we looked into it, was that the cost would be astronomical. So originally we'd scrapped the idea of getting any in-the-wild footage. We'd decided, if possible, to show them on the end of a line instead.

Ascension Island, a volcanic speck of land next to the mid-Atlantic ridge, halfway between Brazil and Angola, was our base for that scene. We took off from RAF Brize Norton (just months before this flight was suspended) and eight hours later landed just south of the equator. And in no time at all we'd confirmed the special richness of the water here. Day two saw me taking four and a half hours to bring in a 248lb yellowfin tuna, something that still takes some believing. Having recovered from that, it was time to go after the six-gills.

Just before nightfall, with land visible as a grey smudge on the moving horizon, we anchored up on the edge of the drop-off. I weighted a hunk of dead fish with a big lump of rock and lowered it 300 feet to the bottom. Then it was a case of concentrating on the rod-tip and correlating its movement with the movement of the boat, and being alert for anything anomalous. This came, eventually, in the form of an out-of-synch nod, followed by what looked like a slightly increased bend. The boat was equipped with a fighting chair, for marlin anglers, but I was fishing 'stand-up' style, so I quickly transferred the rod to the harness that I was already wearing in readiness. From the look of the rod, the consensus was that there was something there, so I started winding down, to set the big circle hook. It was like winding tight to the ocean floor, which then started moving.

For the next forty minutes I shuffled and staggered back and forth along the transom as the boat pitched up and down in the swell. The rod had become a tightly compressed spring, transmitting force equally to me and to the fish. It was one of those situations where the weakest link is not a swivel or a crimp or a knot or the 130lb main line, but the person attached to the rod. In my mind I had a picture of a foot slipping and me being catapulted over the side. So it was good to know that the deck hand was behind me, holding on to my belt, as insurance against that happening. It wasn't that the fish was running; it was just the sheer weight, like trying to winch up a grand piano. The drag was almost fully locked, but even so I had to nudge the lever forward a fraction, and use my fingers to hold the spool when raising the rod. In this way, inch by inch, I put line onto the reel, only to lose it again. But somehow, almost imperceptibly, the amount of line on the reel grew. The swivel at the end of the leader appeared above the surface and gloved hands grabbed the coated wire. A couple more minutes and a grey blunt-nosed beast with a long, sinuous tail was secured at the back of the boat. It was about fourteen feet long and 1,100 pounds. We had our six-gill!

Over the next three nights I had three more, the biggest around 1,300 pounds. To two of these fish we attached special tags that would log temperature, light, and, most importantly, depth. These tags would eventually pop to the surface and relay that information to a satellite, helping to increase understanding of these rarely seen creatures. To complete the work-out I also caught two Galapagos sharks, which look very similar to bull sharks, the biggest around ten feet long and 500 pounds, and a surprise tiger shark, now a rarity in these waters. This was a huge male, twelve or thirteen feet long and weighing perhaps 900 pounds, which is about as big as the males grow.

But most of these fish never made it into the program, because we found a solution for our underwater six-gill shots.

There was a deep-diving submersible based on the island of Roatán in the Caribbean, just off the coast of Honduras and right next to the Cayman Trench. But this was not the kind of vessel that came complete with a mother ship and business-class seats. This was home-made by a young American expat who, I was told, built his first sub in his parents' garden when he was a teenager, out of plumbing parts. I was given the option to politely decline, but our research team were quietly confident and there was already a collective excitement in the air. From the comfort of an airy office I said yes, and the countdown started.

Although six-gills live in perpetual darkness, they are known to migrate upward in the water column at night. During the daytime they would be beyond the range of the sub, so the plan was to go down after sunset. I don't mind admitting that my apprehension was already pretty high, and this cranked it up another notch, but it's that basic principle of fishing again: the importance of the right time. As for the right place, we were governed by the desirability of staying safe and alive. The Cayman Trench goes down nearly five miles (to 25,000 feet), but the sub is designed to operate only to a depth of half a mile, or a little more (3,000 feet). So we would stick to the upper part of the slope.

Bait, when you're hoping to find a carnivore, needs to be some kind of meat. Arriving during the day to give the sub a once-over, we were just in time to help its designer and pilot, Karl Stanley, lash a dead pig to a simple wooden frame that he had bolted to the front of the vessel.

It was also time to try the passenger quarters for size. Entering the top hatch I lowered myself into a vertical space made from two steel spheres welded together. This is where Karl stands when he's driving. Then it was a crouch and an awkward feet-forward shimmy through a knee-high entrance into a second chamber. Hunched forward on the bench seat, I looked out at the friendly faces on the other side of the convex viewport as I tried to imagine what it was going to be like with sixty atmospheres of pressure on the other side: nearly 900 pounds pushing against every square inch. I was still thinking about this when I got out, as I squinted at the rubber seal in the entrance hatch. From my days of rebuilding motorbikes, I know how crucial it is to keep O-rings scrupulously clean, if you want liquids to stay out of places where they shouldn't be. Karl clocked me doing this and read my mind.

'It doesn't matter about that,' he said, adding by way of explanation that the metal surfaces would be pressing together so hard that the seal would be redundant. The four-inch-thick acrylic window in front of me would also compress and shrink, pushing further into its beveled seating.

Despite all this, part of me, of course, couldn't wait. The thought of where we were planning to go, and what we were hoping to see, made me dizzy. When the time came to board for real, I was joined up front by Steve Shearman, whose idea this had been. Steve was the director of this episode, but there was no way he could direct from the surface, since there was no communication of any kind with the sub. There was also no way we could get a third person in that space, so Steve hefted the camera, plus spare batteries and memory cards, and told cameraman Ross Hamilton to get a good night's sleep: it would be his turn tomorrow.

In the dying light we slipped away from the dock and crossed the surface of the shallow bay. My domed port was already submerged, allowing just intermittent splashy glimpses of evening sky, but the hatch remained open for our last taste of fresh air. After a few minutes we were crossing the reef. Then the reef dropped away. A couple of minutes later we stopped. Karl closed the hatch and flooded the ballast compartments, and down we went. He had weighed us and our kit beforehand, and adjusted onboard weighting to make the four-ton vessel just fifteen pounds negatively buoyant when it had no air in the ballast, which gave a gentle but purposeful rate of descent. Looking out through the port I saw illuminated flecks and particles drifting upward. At a depth of fifty feet there was a dull percussive thud. Before setting off, out of curiosity, we'd tied a sealed metal bottle to the outside. Like the sub it contained air at atmospheric pressure. Unlike the sub, it had just collapsed into two dimensions.

Reaching the bottom took forty-five minutes. Through the porthole I saw a sloping white moonscape with protruding black rocks. Karl maneuvered for a minute to find a place that was a bit more horizontal, and we landed. He told us not to expect to see anything for three or four hours, but tonight turned out to be unusual. We'd not long switched to red lights, which are invisible to six-gills, when a pale, huge shape drifted by, on the periphery of the light . . . but then everything went quiet.

I felt something nudge me in the back, and Karl passed me a small black box with a simple digital display. 'This number here should be between 16 and 24,' he said. 'When it gets low, crack a little oxygen.' With that he passed through a metal cylinder with a knurled tap, then curled up in the tiny space behind us. 'If anything happens, hit my foot. I'll be right here.'

It shouldn't have seemed strange that he was settling down to sleep. Underwater is his second home. It's not a lot different from dozing in a bivvy, waiting for the buzzer to go.

But his laid-back air is misleading: he is single-minded and passionate about what he does to an extent that is truly rare. When I'd asked how he'd ended up building and piloting submarines, he'd replied, 'I read a book when I was eight.' And I sensed there was no likelihood that the novelty would ever wear off.

Steve and I, meanwhile, struggled to process this new experience. The red light made me think of a campfire in the desert, and such was the clarity outside that it appeared like air, a night without stars. It was almost possible to imagine opening the hatch and going out for a walk. But then a reality check: out there the air in a pair of human lungs would compress to almost nothing, about the volume of a cigarette packet. It was quite a thing to contemplate, as we sat waiting in the belly of our benevolent metal beast.

Water ran down the chilly metal walls. I knew that it couldn't be salt water, because any leak and we'd already be history. But I tasted it anyway. It was condensed vapor from our breath. This contemplation of water made me aware that I needed to pee, and I couldn't put it off any longer. I located one of the sealable bags that is provided for this purpose, and tried to work out with Steve if there was any way we could reconfigure for this purpose. He ended up tucking into a fetal position behind me while I attempted to kneel, at which point Karl woke up, because our shifting was making the boat rock. We apologized and explained – and this was when the sharks turned up. Like sinuous red airships, they floated into view, circling the sub and bumping it, disappearing and reappearing then disappearing again, keeping us on the edge of our seat. But they never fully closed in on the bait. Eventually they went away, and it was time to surface.

A squirt of air into the ballast compartments and we

started moving. Then some forward thrust and we were following the slope upward. In such ultra-clear water it felt like low-level flying, but in tranquil slow motion. Imperceptibly the gradient steepened, until we were rising alongside the face of the reef – some of it now vertical, some overhanging, a fantastical architecture of white limestone. We arrived at the dock in the small hours of the morning. Our voyage had lasted eight and a half hours.

The next night Ross joined me in the ringside seat. We sat for hours without seeing a thing, other than the shrimps and isopods – like foot-long wood lice – that came to check out the bait. Time slowed to a crawl. With nothing to distract me, I kept thinking about surfacing to a warm bed, but the hands on my watch barely moved. The night finished as a blank, and we ascended vertically through the water column with the lights off, rocking gently in the darkness. I lost myself in a reverie that was broken by a sudden tipping and lurching, and the fear that we would flip over and plunge back down. It was the sign that we were approaching the surface.

On our way back to the dock Karl wondered if we might have been in a dead zone, a place with no water circulation to spread the scent. Down on the bottom the horizons are short, and it was possible we'd been in a gully. A case of the wrong place, in other words . . .

And that was the end of the time we'd booked, other than a shallow dive the next night, when underwater cameraman Florian Graner would get footage of me in the sub from the outside. But Steve wasn't satisfied. Yes, we'd filmed big sharks up close, but we hadn't seen one feeding. Ross and I had to go down again.

Karl decided to go a bit deeper, but the topography is complex. There is always a random element to where you end up, and when the depth gauge went past the 2,000-foot mark, the bottom was still not in sight. Then we saw a black mountainside ahead of us, and Karl halted our descent. He'd spotted a pale shape: a tiny platform carpeted in sand, smaller than the footprint of our sub. He was coming in to land.

How do you rank these moments, these places? People ask me to do it all the time: the most scary, the most dangerous, the most memorable – and I mumble, and feel somehow fraudulent because I can't give a clear answer. But there is always a shortlist. And if I were asked to pick the most dramatic place I have fished, this unmapped ledge would be among the memories that would spool in my mind's eye. To our left was near-vertical rock; to our right and behind us was the abyss. The depth gauge read 2,150 feet, just short of a vertical half-mile. We switched to red light and all this shrank to an intimate rock-garden, almost within touching distance.

As always, the shrimps were quickly on the scene, drawn by invisible tendrils of scent. Next came the isopods, flying through the water and clumsily bumping into my window, then burying their heads inside the pig's flesh and fanning clouds of particles into the water with their tails. Time passed, carrying a charge of anticipation.

The face appeared from nowhere, out of blackness. Then a body longer than the sub slid past. The shark was circling us, trying to read the scent gradient. Now it was coming from the left, angling down. It went past the bait but somehow turned sharply towards us. The eye flashed white as the eyeball rolled back, to protect a wide black pupil that never sees daylight. Then it bit down. For several seconds it rolled left and right, rocking the sub as its teeth sawed into flesh. Just three feet away, the camera also rolled. We had our capture, this time on a memory card rather than a hook, but the basic principles were the same: right bait, right place, right time – plus meticulous attention to gear and procedure, which turned the opportunity into a result.

And there's something here too, I think, about commitment. How much do you want to see that fish? How important is it? In other circumstances I might have wandered up to that dock and thought, There's no way I'm going down in that thing – I'll go and have a gentle snorkel on the reef instead. But I would have missed one of the most mind-expanding experiences of my life. Sometimes to get the big one, you have to go the metaphorical extra mile. Or, in this case, the real extra half-mile.

Afterword

Well, I tried to pick it all apart, but it got tangled up again. Perhaps if I strip away the context and examples, it will be clearer. So here it is in its boiled-down form, the essence of how I fish.

Remember: it's all about **right bait, right place, right time**. So really think these through, especially the right place – the right water, and the right location in that water.

Remember: **you may only get one opportunity**, so you must make that opportunity count.

Remember that **fish are wild animals**. Approach the water with stealth. Don't scare them away before you start fishing – they might be right underneath your feet.

Look at the water. Really look at it. Read the surface to build a picture of what is happening below.

Think like a fish. Where would you be if you were a fish? Where would you feel comfortable and safe, and have access to food?

Remember that **less time can be more**. It's all about fishing effectively, not just putting in the hours. Sometimes it's even good to stop and give the water a rest. (This is especially true if you're putting lures through the same pool or stretch.)

Do your research. Talk to other anglers and weigh up what you hear. Triangulate between sources, to work out what's reliable and what isn't. A lot of successful angling is down to detective work.

Listen to your gut. As you become more experienced, your instincts will become more reliable.

Gear up for the biggest fish that you may hook. There's no point hooking the fish of a lifetime if it becomes the one that got away. Don't be embarrassed about using heavy tackle, if that is what's required.

Plan how you will get the fish in, before you cast. Think through all the 'what ifs.' Doing this when the fish is on the line could be too late.

Be constantly ready: something may happen at any moment – including on the first cast. Don't let your guard down, but don't focus too intently on the fish.

Fish with confidence. If you're not confident, find out why that is and do something about it.

Be opportunistic. Be prepared to change your plans if an unexpected opportunity arises.

Be able to tie a few knots well. Practice at home, before arriving at the water. A basic knot tied well is more use than a fancy knot tied badly.

Fish with attention to detail. Is the hook sharp? Is the line good? Are knots tied to complete satisfaction? There's no excuse for losing a fish through human error.

Be familiar with your gear, especially reel controls and how these work. Rehearse mentally what you will do if a fish takes, so you don't have to think about it at the time.

Practice essential techniques before arriving at the water. Casting accurately, and sometimes quickly, can be the key to success.

Be inventive. Don't be afraid to try something new or different from what everyone else is doing. Even a non-result is a result, because it teaches you something.

Don't assume that having more lines in the water automatically improves your chances. It's often better to fish one outfit with concentration.

If nothing is happening, **weigh the benefits of stay put versus move**. It's always a difficult one, but don't let laziness be the deciding factor. Sometimes the best option is to pack up and come back with renewed energy.

Learn from your mistakes. Don't let the same thing happen again. Try to eliminate all human error.

Look after your fish, and the world they live in. Professing to care about animals but not caring about their environment is an inconsistent attitude.

Think about getting in the water. Or you may prefer not to, on the wholly justifiable basis that diving and snorkeling can demystify fishing. It's a case of personal outlook.

Keep a fishing diary. It's a reliable extension to your mental database, and will help you to get more out of your fishing.

Remember that **you never cast into the same river twice**. Or the same lake. What worked yesterday won't necessarily work today, so don't get set in your ways.

And **keep enjoying it**. If enjoyment is missing it is time to quit. But it should also be a struggle. The two are not incompatible.

Teach somebody else to fish, to help secure the future of the underwater world.

These are the things I'm telling myself when I'm fishing. It's mostly not a conscious process, but happening quietly in the background. Essentially it's fishing thoughtfully and actively, rather than automatically and passively.

I finish with my hope that, whoever you are and whatever your level of experience, something in these pages will help to bring a special fish onto your line – and into your hands – that wouldn't have come along otherwise.

Appendix:
Keeping Legal and Good Practice

To fish any public water in the US (inland or salt water) it is, in most cases, necessary to buy a fishing license. These are issued by individual states, and are easily bought online or at authorized outdoor goods stores and tackle shops. Guides and charters will also commonly assist with licenses, as part of the package.

Depending on the state, licenses are issued by the Department of Natural Resources or other fish/game/park/wildlife agency. A good place for quickly finding out all necessary information, wherever you are, is the US Fish & Wildlife Service: fws.gov/fishing/FishingLicense.html. Alternatively go to the takemefishing.org website (also vamosapescar.org) run by the nonprofit Recreational Boating and Fishing Foundation (RBFF).

Licenses can be one-day, short-term, annual, or lifetime. Discounts are often available for veterans and others, and those under sixteen are commonly exempt. Revenues raised go towards fish and environment conservation.

Different states have their own rules and regulations. However, even if taking fish from the water is permitted, all anglers who are concerned about maintaining fish populations (apart from invasive species) should voluntarily practice catch and release (see Chapter 21). Likewise, certain techniques that are legal in some states, such as trotlines (long lines), jug lines (lines fished under multiple buoys) and limb lines (unattended set lines attached to tree branches), don't really have a place in twenty-first-century recreational fishing. And those practicing catfish noodling (hand fishing), in states where this is permitted, should ideally return the fish immediately to the same water. To learn more about best practices, visit fishsmart.org and releasense.org. More information can be found at sportfishingconservancy.com (the Sportfishing Conservancy) and asafishing.org (American Sportfishing Association).

See also National Park Service (nps.gov/subjects/fishing/fishing-regulations.htm) for fishing in national parks and gulfcouncil.org for fishing in the Gulf of Mexico.

As a final point, when searching for information online, you may (in the spirit of independent thought and action, which this book seeks to foster) wish to consider using an alternative to the search engine that most people use as their automatic default. There are other search engines that don't collect or share personal information, but instead only collect data about search terms, not linked to the user. See, for example, duckduckgo.com.

Glossary

This is not an exhaustive list of angling terms, but it aims to give the basic meaning of terms used in this book.

Action. The feel of a rod, based on the shape it makes when under tension. A fast-action rod will mostly bend towards the tip. A slow- or through-action rod will bend right through to the butt.

Artificial. See *lure*.

Bail arm (sometimes **bale arm**). The metal hoop (also called the pick-up) on a *fixed-spool reel*, which flips between open and closed positions. When open, line can spill off the spool. When closed, line can be retrieved. Normally closes automatically when the reel handle is turned, and incorporates a roller to reduce line wear. Trying to cast with the bail arm closed is very embarrassing, even if no one is watching. If you're using a heavy lead it can also be dangerous.

Baitcaster reel. Reel with gear-operated rotating spool, mounted on top of the rod handle so the thumb can brake the spool on the cast.

Bait elastic. Thin elastic used to attach a soft natural bait to a hook, where the hook might otherwise not hold the bait or damage it to the point where it will easily fall off.

Baitrunner reel/mechanism. See *freespool reel.*

Barbless hook. Exactly that, and now widely used. Other hooks have a micro barb. A DIY option is to crush down the barb with pliers, leaving a small bump. Will safely bring a fish in, but extra care should be taken not to allow the line to fall slack.

Boilies. Spherical baits made from ingredients bound together with egg, boiled to make them hard and resistant to break-up. Fished on a *hair rig.* Shop-bought boilies are between 6mm and 26mm in diameter, but for mahseer fishing in South India I made millet paste boilies the size of my fist.

Braid (braided line, multifilament). Modern braided and woven lines are made from man-made fibers with exceptional tensile strength. Much easier to use than heavy *monofilament*, being much thinner for the same breaking strain, which increases reel capacity. They are also more supple and have zero stretch. Against that, they are less resistant to abrasion and more expensive, but the higher cost is offset by their being very long-lasting.

Centerpin reel. The simplest type of reel, consisting of a drum rotating on a spindle. Ideally suited to *trotting*, they also give a uniquely direct sense of connection to a hooked fish. Rarely seen since the arrival of mass-produced *fixed-spool reels*, which are much easier to cast with.

Circle hook. Hook pattern where the point is turned in towards the hook shank. Looks like it shouldn't work, but in fact very effective in some circumstances. The hook is set by allowing the line to tighten, or by slowly pulling tight. (Pulling back quickly in response to a take will normally bump the hook clear of the mouth, so you must override this reflex.) Main advantage is that it avoids deep-hooking, and normally hooks neatly in the corner of the mouth. See *J-hook*.

Coracle. Lightweight circular boat traditionally made from a wooden frame covered with animal skin. Once used by fishermen in Wales, and still used in South India, where the skin is now woven plastic sacking waterproofed with tar.

Crimp. Metal sleeve used to fix multi-strand wire (or heavy *nylon/fluoro*) to a hook or swivel.

Deadbait. Normally a dead fish or part of a dead fish.

Drag. Important feature of most reels. Adjust friction so drag will slip before the line breaks. Correct setting is crucial for strike; then may need to adjust as fish is brought in. With experience, strike drag can be set by feel, or use a known pre-set, or use a spring balance.

Dug-out canoe. A wooden canoe made from a single tree trunk.

Fixed-spool reel. Another name for spinning reel. (Also known as egg beater in Australia and coffee grinder in South Africa.) The most common kind of reel for most fishing. An ingenious design whereby the axis of the non-rotating spool is (more or less) parallel to the rod, so that the line, when released, will spill off the spool and give easy, long, accurate casts.

Float tube. Also called belly boat or kick boat. Inflatable seat-like fishing platform, propelled by fins on the angler's legs, which work below the surface. Not advisable where fish share the water with crocs.

Fluorocarbon (fluoro). Clear fishing line similar in appearance to nylon *monofilament* but denser and heavier. More abrasion resistant than mono and almost invisible in water, but more memory (springiness) and less forgiving of poor knot tying. Good leader material (except for surface lures). Some spoolable fluoro is available, as is fluoro-coated mono.

Fly-fishing. Use of extremely lightweight *lures* that mimic insects or small fish. Because these flies are so lightweight, they have to be cast using special heavy line, and rods that are specially designed to handle these lines. Fishing flies are normally constructed from pieces of feather, fur, and synthetic fabric, bound to the hook by thread. Sometimes lead/brass/tungsten weight or buoyant foam is added, along with refinements such as weed guards and plastic eyes. At the other extreme, the simplest fly I have used was a strip of rag torn from my T-shirt, fished on six feet of nylon line attached to a cane. Twitched through the water in small rapid jerks, the rag transforms into a remarkably good likeness of a small fish. When worked along the edges of fallen tree trunks, this can be a killer method for Amazonian peacock bass.

Freelining. Fishing with just a hook on the end of the line and nothing else. The ultimate in simplicity (apart from a handline). Advantages: quick and easy to set up, only one knot as a potential weak point. Disadvantages: hard to cast light baits, hard to detect some bites. Should not be used if any risk of fish taking the bait undetected.

Freespool reel. *Fixed-spool reel* concept originally developed by Shimano in the 1970s (marketed as 'Baitrunner' reels) whereby a fish can take line, against minimal resistance, with the *bail arm* closed. This is achieved through use of a secondary drag mechanism, with a separate rotating control, which is engaged by means of a lever. Switching back to the main drag is by means of the same lever, or by turning the reel handle. Very useful in running water, when resistance can be precisely matched to current strength. Removes any need to fish with an open bail arm, which risks tangles.

Hair rig. Revolutionary method of rigging, now with many variations and refinements, whereby the bait (usually a *boilie*) is not mounted on the hook but suspended from the hook shank by a short 'hair' of *leader* material, formed by using a knotless knot. Allows more natural behavior of hookbait and gives improved hook-up rates.

High sticking. Holding the rod too close to the vertical when playing a fish. Ideally the butt of the rod and the line should make an angle of about 90 degrees. Clearly this angle will decrease and increase somewhat when *pumping* the rod to bring a fish in, but the angle should never be too acute when the rod is under load. The greatest risk of this is when the fish is in close, and the consequence can be a broken rod-tip, and a lost fish. (Can also refer to a specialized *fly-fishing* technique, for presenting a fly in fast water at close range.)

Hook length. The short length of line to which the hook is tied. Often a different material from the main line.

J-hook. The conventional fish-hook shape, like the letter J. But in the same way that typography gives us many variants of the letter J, so too does hook design: long shank, wide gape, offset point, thick wire, thin wire, bent shank . . . adding up to a huge number of different patterns.

Jig. A *lure* comprising a plastic body threaded onto a hook that has an integral weight near the eye. This can be lowered from a boat and moved vertically up and down, or cast and twitched along the bottom.

Landing net. Net on a handle for safely enclosing the fish and bringing it ashore, or into the boat.

Leader. The short length of line on the end of the main line, to which the hook or *lure* is attached. Normally a different material from the main line, with different properties – e.g., more supple, more bite resistant, less visible. A short leader attached directly to a hook is called a *hook length*.

Legering (also **ledgering**). Any technique where a lead or other weight holds the line on the bottom.

Long line. A commercial fishing method comprising a length of strong line with shorter hook lengths at intervals. Widely used for marine species, but also used in rivers in some countries. Can be set to fish near the surface, using floats, or on the bottom.

Long-trotting. See *trotting*.

Lure. An artificial lure is any non-edible bait that mimics a small fish or other food item, such as a frog or crab. Some, such as modern soft plastic baits, are very lifelike. Others, such as bar spoons, *spinnerbaits* and buzzbaits, don't resemble any known fish but are more like caricatures, sending out exaggerated vibrations and visual signals to call the attention of a predator. Some are very low-tech. In the Solomon Islands I caught a trevally on a piece of white leaf, taken to the bottom using a rock then swum to the surface on a handline; and in the Amazon I caught peacock bass on a piece of rag torn from a T-shirt, twitched alongside fallen tree trunks.

Monofilament (mono, nylon). What most people think of when they think of fishing line. Literally a single, clear filament of nylon. Classed according to diameter and breaking strain. Different brands vary in terms of stretch, memory (the tendency to hold a twist), hardness, color, etc. See *braid*.

Multiplier reel. British name for the 'conventional'/casting reel, which is the type of reel I normally use, mounted on top of the rod. (Australians call it an 'overhead' reel.) Most commonly used in salt water, and so called because one turn of the handle produces more turns of the spool, by means of gears. They take some practice to master, because if the spool rotates too quickly on the cast, it can overrun and cause a 'bird's nest,' but modern reels have built-in brakes, which make this less of an issue. Better for bringing in heavy fish than a *fixed-spool reel*.

Nylon. See *monofilament*.

Outrigger. Long arm projecting from the side of a big-game boat, fitted with a cord-and-pulley mechanism carrying line clips. Enables multiple lures (commonly four) to be *trolled* in a wide formation without risk of tangling.

Particles, particle baits. Small hookbaits used in conjunction with a scatter of free offerings. The best known is probably sweetcorn. Nuts and seeds must be properly prepared (soaked and cooked) so they don't swell inside the fish's stomach. Or buy pre-prepared.

Plumbing. Use of a lead weight, normally in conjunction with a float, to measure the depth of water. Best method is to thread a running lead (then a bead) onto the line, then attach a large float to the end. After casting, pull the float down to the weight, then release a foot of line at a time until the float appears at the surface. (This won't work in strong current. Here the best option is *sonar*.) Dragging with a weight can also give information about the nature of the bottom: where there is sand, gravel, rock, silt and weed.

Popper. Floating *lure* with a flat or concave head, designed to make loud popping and gurgling sounds when retrieved across the surface in a series of sharp jerks.

Pumping (as in **pumping the rod**). Trying to turn a reel against strong resistance will not work. To bring in a big fish, you have to use the rod. Bring in a few feet of line by pulling the rod back (but not too far) then wind down as you drop the rod forward again. Repeat. Keep tension on the fish all the time – a very common mistake is to let the line go slack when winding down, which can lead to the hook falling out. (The hook is sometimes not fully home in the early stages, but slowly pulls into a secure hold.)

Running lead. A weight that holds the line in place on the bottom but which allows a fish to pull the line without moving or feeling the weight (either because the weight has a hole bored through it or because the line passes through an eye or an attached swivel). The set-up as a whole is known as a 'running rig.'

Shock leader. A length of heavy line (about one and a half rod lengths) between the main line and the *hook length*, used to prevent a break-off when casting a heavy weight long distances. When casting, the near end of the shock leader needs to be on the reel, so none of the main line is subjected to the stress of casting.

Sliding float. As the name implies it slides up the line, normally because of a hole running through it. Stopped at a pre-set depth by a stop knot on the line with a sliding bead below it. Allows float-fishing in water that is deeper than the length of the rod, since the stop-knot easily passes through the rings and onto the reel.

Sonar. Method of detecting objects underwater by sending out sound waves and picking up the echoes, as used by dolphins ('echo location'). Man-made sonars are very useful for mapping depths from a boat ('echo sounding'), and most can also detect fish (may be marketed as 'fishfinders'). Sophisticated models also have GPS and 'side scan,' which shows objects such as sunken tree trunks to the side of the boat as illuminated 3D shapes with dark shadows. The simplest sonars are the size of a waterproof flashlight.

Spinnerbait. *Lure* with a wire frame that somewhat resembles a miniature coat hanger. On one arm it carries one or more flashing spoon-like blades; on the other is a weighted, inward-turned single hook, adorned with a trailing skirt of colorful plastic strands. Can be fished through weed without snagging.

Spinning. Common term for *lure* fishing. So called because many early metal lures (spinners) would spin on the end of the line, sending out vibrations and flashes of light.

Tag end. When tying a knot, this is the shorter of the two pieces of line emerging from the knot, usually a few inches long. After tightening the knot, the tag end should be snipped close (but not too close) to the knot.

Terminal tackle. All the bits and bobs on the end of the main reel line. As well as the hook (sometimes more than one), this may include items such as: float, weight/s, swivel/s, *leader*, *hook length*, wire *trace*. The number of permutations, for different types of fishing, is endless.

Test curve. A measure of rod flexibility. The amount of force needed to pull the rod-tip into a position where it is making a 90-degree angle with the butt. Most early carp rods had a test curve around 1.5lb. For modern carp fishing (longer range, heavier casting weights, bigger fish) it's more commonly 2.25–3.5lb. Lure-fishing rods are normally rated in terms of casting weight. Heavier saltwater rods are rated in terms of line strength: 30-, 50- and 130lb-class.

Tippet. The thinnest and very end piece of a fly-fishing *leader*.

Top shot. Top shotting is the increasingly common practice, mostly in salt water, of combining *braid* with *mono* (or *fluoro*). Normally the braid is loaded onto the reel first, then joined to a top shot of mono. Among its benefits, it allows the use of smaller-capacity reels than previously possible.

Touch-legering (also **touch-ledgering**). Possibly the most sensitive bite detector is a human fingertip, resting on the line above the reel. It's possible to fish a single rod like this for several hours.

Trace. *Leader* made from wire, to prevent the fish's teeth biting through it. Used when the target species has cutting teeth, or when another toothy species might investigate.

Trolling. Pulling a *lure* behind a boat. Seeing the bottom with *sonar* helps to troll more effectively.

Trotting. Letting a float go downstream with the current. Most fun with a *centerpin reel*. Once you've got 'quite a lot' of line out, you're long trotting. I caught one of my most memorable childhood fish this way: my first three-pound chub. More recently it has brought goliath tigerfish.

Uptide rod. Saltwater boat-fishing rod designed for casting 'upstream' into the tide, with an anchor-like grip lead and a slack line. Longer and lighter in action than a conventional boat rod.

Wind-on leader. A long *leader* of thick *monofilament* with a flexible loop at one end made from woven Dacron (Terylene). When joined (using a loop-to-loop cat's paw) to a loop in the end of the main line (formed by a Bimini twist), this thick leader can be wound through the rod rings and onto the reel, which isn't possible if the leader is attached using a swivel. Makes line management much easier when a big fish comes in close.

Acknowledgments

This book is a spoonful of boiled-down fish soup, in the best tradition of bouillabaisse. Many, many people contributed to the pot, both knowingly and unknowingly, and, while a few of them are mentioned in the text, it would be impossible to list all of my teachers, informants and collaborators, but my thanks are due to you all. Among those helping me to stir the mix were the shadowy companions in the background of some of these stories – occasionally heard as 'voices off' – who, by asking sometimes obvious questions, helped to fish insights into the light. These people are the directors, camera operators and other crew members who, in recent years, have had the job of turning my scrappy exploits into educational entertainment, on behalf of the Bristol-based television production company Icon Films. Meanwhile, for helping to transform this book from a dimly glimpsed thing under the surface into something I can at last hold in my hands, I'm indebted to my agent Julian Alexander and my editors Renée Sedliar at Da Capo and Alan Samson at Weidenfeld & Nicolson. Also at Da Capo I am grateful to Bob Pigeon for casting a US angler's eye over the text.

A version of Chapter 13 was first published in *Scuba*, the magazine of the British Sub-Aqua Club. Reproduced with permission. The quotation from Sun-tzu's *The Art of War* is from the translation by John Minford (Penguin 2002).

Index

adrenaline, 18, 22–3, 96
agoutis, 19
aikido, 102
Alaska, 56
alligator gar (*Atractosteus spatula*), 28, 64, 136
all-tackle records, 81
Amazon, river system, 11, 18–23, 25–7, 34–5, 45, 49, 51, 95, 153, 163, 165, 168, 183, 195, 244
    commercial fishing, 26, 34
    mãe d'água (mother of the water), 155
    water levels, 209, 214
anacondas, 25, 130
angling partnerships, 164–5
Angling Trust, 23–8
Araguaia River, 34
arapaima (*Arapaima gigas*), 11, 25–8, 78, 94–101, 105, 119–20, 152, 182–3
Arctic char, 129
arowana (*Osteoglossum bicirrhosum*), 166

Ascension Island, 82, 185, 199, 224
atmospheric pressure, 175, 209
Australians, indigenous, 198, 200
bait
    bait fishing, 132–41, 160–3
    boilies, 240
    breadcrust, floating, 7–8
    carp baits, 207, 209
    deadbait, 57, 78, 133, 209, 241
    dog biscuits, 69, 209
    livebait, 115, 168
    particle bait, 245
    potatoes, 160–1
Banbibi, goddess, 155
basketball, 102
bathyscopes, 59
'BB,' *see* Watkins-Pitchford, Denys
beliefs and superstitions, 154–6
benzene, ring structure of, 176–7

fishing diaries, *see* notebooks
fishing gear, 30, 38–9
  advances in, 184–5
  and angler's skill, 80–1
  and attention to detail,
    187–90
  buffalo test, 184
  float tubes, 103, 142–3, 146,
    241
  gorges, 48–9
  hook sharpness, 188–9
  light versus heavy, 73, 77–83,
    186
  line breakages, 80
  line condition, 189
  multiplier reels, 38, 78, 83,
    86, 105, 137, 150, 245–6
  poppers, 82, 245
  rods, 150–3
  test curve, 150, 248
  see also hooks; knots
fishing techniques
  bait fishing, 132–41, 160–3
  basket fishing, 48
  big circle technique, 74–5
  bow fishing, 45, 6
  creep and drift, 104–5
  dumping the line, 145
  figure-eight technique, 74–5
  fly-fishing, 96–7, 102–6, 189,
    242
  freelining, 7, 160, 242
  hair rigs, 162–3, 242
  handlining, 182–3, 185–6
  multiple rods, 132, 135–41
  noodling, 213–19

poison, 48
spear fishing, 46
spider-web fishing, 47–8
Fitzroy River, 199
floodplain drainage, 28
Florida, 78

Ganges, river, 155, 182
German and Swiss anglers,
    197–8
giant salamanders, 129
giant snakeheads, 129
Göz, Daniel, 119
Graner, Florian, 230
grayling, 103
groupers
  goliath grouper (*Epinephelus
    itajara*), 79
  Queensland groper
    (*Epinephelus lanceolatus*),
    115, 117
Gulf of Carpentaria, 115
Guyana, 33–5, 94, 106

Hamilton, Ross, 227, 230
harpoon heads, 45
Hasegawa, Atsushi, 103–4
Hemingway, Ernest, 103, 185
Heraclitus, 58
high sticking, 144, 243
Himalayan foothills, 85, 129,
    180
hippopotamuses, 43
hooks, 49–50
  barbless, 240
  circle hooks, 240–1

Index

Index